GREEN LIGHT FOR THE TOEIC® TEST

Maiko Tsuchiya
Yoshie Shimai
Samuel Paolo M. Adamos

GREEN LIGHT FOR THE TOEIC® TEST

Maiko Tsuchiya / Yoshie Shimai / Samuel Paolo M. Adamos

© 2016 Cengage Learning K.K.

ALL RIGHTS RESERVED. No part of this work covered by the copyright herein may be reproduced, transmitted, stored or used in any form or by any means—graphic, electronic, or mechanical, including but not limited to photocopying, recording, scanning, digitizing, taping, Web distribution, information networks, or information storage and retrieval systems—without the prior written permission of the publisher.

The TOEIC® Test Directions (pages 9-13, 15, 16, 105-109, 111, 112):
Copyright © 2015 Educational Testing Service. www.ets.org

The TOEIC® Test Directions are reprinted by permission of Educational Testing Service, the copyright owner. All other information contained within this publication is provided by Cengage Learning K.K. No endorsement of any kind by Educational Testing Service should be inferred.

Photo Credits:
front cover: © SGM/age fotostock; 9, 104: © Educational Testing Service; 9: (1) © Bloomimage/Corbis, (2) © michaeljung/iStock/Thinkstock; 22: © ajkkafe/iStock/Thinkstock; 23: (1) © Elena Elisseeva/iStock/Thinkstock, (2) © Purestock/Thinkstock; 40: © kzenon/iStock/Thinkstock; 41: (1) © mihalis_a/iStock/Thinkstock, (2) © aerogondo/iStock/Thinkstock; 58: © Digital Vision./DigitalVision/Thinkstock; 59: (1) © Martin Poole/DigitalVision/Thinkstock, (2) © Wavebreakmedia Ltd/Wavebreak Media/Thinkstock, (3) © Monkey Business Images/Monkey Business/Thinkstock; 104: (1) © Wavebreakmedia Ltd/Wavebreak Media/Thinkstock, (2) © DamianPalus/iStock/Thinkstock

For permission to use material from this textbook or product, e-mail to **elt@cengagejapan.com**

ISBN: 978-4-86312-278-9

Cengage Learning K.K.
No. 2 Funato Building 5th Floor
1-11-11 Kudankita, Chiyoda-ku
Tokyo 102-0073
Japan

Tel: 03-3511-4392
Fax: 03-3511-4391

まえがき

「TOEICテストを初めて受けようと思っているのですが、何から勉強を始めたらよいですか。どうやって勉強をしたらよいか分かりません」

　これは大学生からよく受ける質問ですが、皆さんも同じようなことを考えてはいませんか。このテキストは、そういう皆さんを応援するために作成されました。「TOEICテストを受けるぞ」と決心すると、多くの人が過去問題や模擬問題を解くことに着手しますが、気を付けるべきことや知っておくべきことに意識を払うことなく、解き進めている人をよく見かけます。なるべく早く目標の点数に到達するためには、効率の良い学習方法が必要です。このテキストは、まず頭にインプットすべき内容で構成されています。各ユニットのキーポイントをしっかり押さえながら、効率良く着実に学習を進めましょう。

　また、このテキストはTOEICテストにも必要な基本的な語句で構成されています。各ユニット冒頭のVocabularyでは、英語と日本語の対応がパッと見てすぐ目に入るよう、また片方を隠しながらのセルフチェックできるよう、英語と和訳を横並びに配列するという工夫をしています。あなたが「単語や熟語を覚えるのは苦手」というタイプの場合、覚え方を工夫してみてはどうでしょう？何度も見たり、書いたり、声を出したり、音声を聞いたり、友人と問題を出し合ったりしながら、自分に合った方法を見つけてください。

　そのほか、このテキストにはActive ReadingやThink-Write-Shareといった、学習仲間と意見を交換したり、声を出したりするアクティビティが組み込まれています。これらも効率の良い学習を促進するために設定されています。一人で黙々と勉強をしていると、大事なことを見逃したり、自身で分かったつもりになったり、何より学習がつまらなくなったりしてしまうことがあります。そうならないためにも友人と一緒に考えたり、声に出して練習したりするのは有効です。相乗効果で学習に勢いがつくよう、積極的に活動を行ってほしいと思います。

　また、2016年5月から導入される新しい出題形式に対応しているので、このテキストを用いて、いち早く新形式のTOEICテスト対策に励んでください。

　最後になりますが、本書の出版に際して、センゲージ ラーニング株式会社の皆様、特に編集の吉田剛氏、株式会社ウィットハウスの古郡あゆみ氏にはご尽力頂きましたことに心より感謝を申し上げます。

著者

Contents

本書の構成と効果的な使い方 ·· 6
TOEIC® テストについて ··· 8

Pre-test ·· 9

Unit 1 Daily Life   名詞と代名詞 ··· 21
　　Listening Section   Part 1　　進行形 (be 動詞 + *doing*) の表現に慣れよう！
　　Reading Section   Part 5 & 6　品詞 1：名詞と代名詞

Unit 2 Health   動詞・形容詞・副詞 ·· 27
　　Listening Section   Part 2　　疑問文への答え方に慣れよう！
　　Reading Section   Part 5 & 6　品詞 2：動詞・形容詞・副詞

Unit 3 Education   時制 1 ··· 33
　　Listening Section   Part 3　　設問のポイントをすばやく押さえてから聞こう！
　　Reading Section   Part 5 & 6　時制（基本時制・進行形）

Unit 4 Travel   時制 2 ··· 39
　　Listening Section   Part 1　　位置関係を示す表現をマスターしよう！
　　Reading Section   Part 5 & 6　完了形

Unit 5 Transportation   前置詞 ··· 45
　　Listening Section   Part 2　　提案・依頼・許可への応答パターンに慣れよう！
　　Reading Section   Part 5 & 6　前置詞

Unit 6 Shopping   接続詞 ·· 51
　　Listening Section   Part 3　　設問の主語を押さえよう！
　　Reading Section   Part 5 & 6　接続詞

Unit 7 Restaurant   不定詞 1 ·· 57
　　Listening Section   Part 1　　人や物の様子・状態を表す定型表現を押さえよう！
　　Reading Section   Part 5 & 6　不定詞 1：to 不定詞の用法

Unit 8 Entertainment 不定詞2 ·· 63
  Listening Section Part 2　　　付加疑問文・否定疑問文への答え方に慣れよう！
  Reading Section　 Part 5 & 6　不定詞2：不定詞をとる動詞

Unit 9 Trouble 動名詞 ··· 69
  Listening Section Part 3　　　会話の流れに沿って設問のヒントを探そう！
  Reading Section　 Part 5 & 6　動名詞

Unit 10 Office 1 分詞 ·· 75
  Listening Section Part 3　　　語句の言い換え（パラフレーズ）を見抜こう！
  Reading Section　 Part 5 & 6　分詞

Unit 11 Office 2 仮定法 ··· 81
  Listening Section Part 3　　　設問パターンを知り、注意点を予測しておこう！
  Reading Section　 Part 5 & 6　仮定法

Unit 12 News 関係代名詞 ··· 87
  Listening Section Part 4　　　キーワードから説明文の種類と大意をつかもう！
  Reading Section　 Part 5 & 6　関係代名詞
  　　　　　　　　　 Part 7　　　キーワードからトピックをすばやくつかもう！

Unit 13 Ads 関係副詞 ·· 95
  Listening Section Part 4　　　設問の中の具体的な語句に注意しよう！
  Reading Section　 Part 5 & 6　関係副詞
  　　　　　　　　　 Part 7　　　マルチ（ダブル）パッセージでは情報を照らし合わせよう！

Post-test ···105

Appendix (人称代名詞の変化表・Glossary) ··116
Pre-/Post-test 解答用紙 ··121

本書の構成と効果的な使い方

本書は全13ユニットで構成され、巻頭にPre-test、巻末にPost-testを掲載しています。

Pre-testとPost-test

Pre-testとPost-testは、本番の4分の1のボリュームですが、TOEICテストにまだあまり慣れていない皆さんがテストの雰囲気をつかむことができるよう、実際のテストと同じ構成をとっています。

> **注意**
> Pre-testとPost-testの音声は、教師用CDだけに収録されています（トラック番号が「T」となっています）。

各ユニットの構成

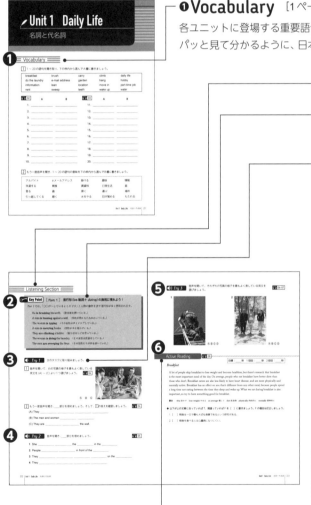

❶ Vocabulary ［1ページ目］
各ユニットに登場する重要語句を学習します。復習のときに、英語と日本語の対応がパッと見て分かるように、日本語の意味を横に書き込むようになっています。

Listening Section ［2～3ページ目］

❷ Key Point 問題を解くときに必ず知っておくべきポイントを学習します。

❸ Try 1 実際に問題を解きながら、❷で学習した内容を確認するために、まずチャレンジする問題です。「気をつけるべき点に意識を払うこと」に集中しやすくするために、実際のTOEICテストより選択肢が少なくなっています（Part 2タイプの問題を除く）。また、並行して英語の音を聞き取る練習として、ディクテーション形式のスクリプト穴埋めタスクが後に続いています。

❹ Try 2 ユニットのテーマおよび❷に関連した英文を聞き、空所に適切な語句を書き入れてスクリプトを完成させます。Try 1よりも空所が多くなっています。

❺ Try 3 ❷で扱っているパートの模擬問題です。本番形式の問題に挑戦しましょう。

❻ Active Reading 目的は「教養として外国の文化や情報を知ること」と「リスニング力とリーディング力の補強」の2つです。リスニング力を高める方法の一つとして、音読は効果的です。さらに、正しく音読ができるようになると意味を理解するスピードも速くなります。ペアやグループでチェックし合ったり、タイムを比較したりしながら楽しく取り組みましょう。

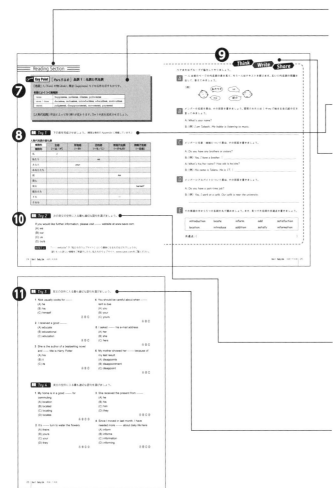

Reading Section [4～6ページ目]

❼ Key Point　Part 5と6対策として、必ず理解しておきたい基礎的な文法事項のまとめです。Unit 12と13にはPart 7対策もあります。

❽ Try 1　❼で得た知識をTOEIC形式の問題を解く際にどのように使えばよいかを練習します。

❾ Think-Write-Share　❼で得た知識を活用する練習を行います。"Share"という語が示すように、ペアやグループのメンバーと一緒に意見を交換しながら取り組みましょう。友人と話すという協同作業で学習をすると、ひとりでやると見過ごすようなことに気付いたり、より良い理解の仕方を発見したりするという効果があります。意見がないと話し合うための材料がありません。"Share"を充実させるためには、まず自分でよく考え (Think)、意見を書いてみること (Write) が大切です。

❿ Try 2　実際に問題を解きながら、❼で学習した内容を確認しましょう。「気をつけるべき点に意識を払うこと」に集中しやすくするために、実際のTOEICテストより選択肢が少なくなっています。

⓫ Try 3　TOEICテストのリーディングセクションのいずれか1つのパートの模擬問題です。本番形式の問題に挑戦しましょう。

音声ファイルの無料ダウンロード

テキスト本体の音声ファイル（ 🎧 のアイコン部分）を無料ダウンロードできます。

http://cengage.jp/elt/Exam/

① 上記URLにアクセス。またはQRコードをスマートフォンなどのリーダーでスキャン（→④へ）
② 本書の表紙画像またはタイトル (GREEN LIGHT FOR THE TOEIC® TEST) をクリック
③ 本書のページで 音声ファイル ボタンをクリック
④ 表示されるファイル名をクリックして音声ファイルをダウンロード

TOEIC® テストについて

TOEICテストとは、Test of English for International Communicationの略称で、英語でのコミュニケーション能力を幅広く評価する世界共通のテストです。TOEICテストは、合格・不合格ではなく、10点から990点のスコアで評価されます。リスニング（45分間、Part 1, 2, 3, 4、全100問）、リーディング（75分間、Part 5, 6, 7、全100問）の2つのセクションで構成されており、どちらもマークシート方式で解答します。2016年5月の公開テストから新形式の問題が加わり、各パートの設問数と内容は以下のようになります。

リスニングセクション （45分間・100問）

Part 1　写真描写問題【6問】	1枚の写真について4つの短い描写文が1度だけ放送されます。描写文は印刷されていません。写真を最も的確に描写している文を選びます。
Part 2　応答問題【25問】	1つの質問または文に対して3つの応答文が1度だけ放送されます。どちらも印刷されていません。3つの選択肢から最も適切な応答文を選びます。
Part 3　会話問題【39問】	2人または3人による会話が1度だけ放送されます。会話は印刷されていません。1つの会話には設問が3つあります。会話を聞いて、印刷されている設問とそれぞれ4つの選択肢を読み、最も適切な答えを選びます。
Part 4　説明文問題【30問】	1人の話者によるアナウンスやニュースのような説明文が1度だけ放送されます。説明文は印刷されていません。1つの説明文には設問が3つあります。説明文を聞いて、印刷されている設問とそれぞれ4つの選択肢を読み、最も適切な答えを選びます。
☺ Part 3とPart 4では、聞いた内容と問題用紙に印刷された図やグラフなどの視覚情報を関連づけて解答する設問も出題されます。（→ pp. 83, 97）	

※一口に英語といっても、英語はいろいろな国で使用されている言語なので、TOEICテストのリスニングセクションのナレーションには、アメリカのほか、イギリス、カナダ、オーストラリアの発音が含まれています。

リーディングセクション （75分間・100問）

Part 5　短文穴埋め問題【30問】	空所が1つ設けられた文を完成させるために、4つの選択肢から最も適切なものを選びます。
Part 6　長文穴埋め問題【16問】	空所が4つ設けられた文書（メールや広告など）を完成させるために、それぞれ4つの選択肢から最も適切なものを選びます。空所の1つは文で埋めます。
Part 7　長文読解問題【54問】	メールや広告、チャットなど、いろいろなタイプの文書が提示されます。その内容に関する複数の設問とそれぞれ4つの選択肢を読み、最も適切な答えを選びます。前半は1つの文書に設問が2～4つ、後半は2つの文書に設問が5つあります。文書内の適切な位置に文を挿入する設問も出題されます。

Pre-test (問題の音声は教師用 CD に収録されています)

LISTENING TEST

In the Listening test, you will be asked to demonstrate how well you understand spoken English. The entire Listening test will last approximately 12 minutes. There are four parts, and directions are given for each part. You must mark your answers on the separate answer sheet. Do not write your answers in your test book.

PART 1

Directions: For each question in this part, you will hear four statements about a picture in your test book. When you hear the statements, you must select the one statement that best describes what you see in the picture. Then find the number of the question on your answer sheet and mark your answer. The statements will not be printed in your test book and will be spoken only one time.

Example

Sample Answer
Ⓐ Ⓑ ● Ⓓ

Statement (C), "They're sitting at a table," is the best description of the picture, so you should select answer (C) and mark it on your answer sheet.

1.

Ⓐ Ⓑ Ⓒ Ⓓ

2.

Ⓐ Ⓑ Ⓒ Ⓓ

GO ON TO THE NEXT PAGE

PART 2

Directions: You will hear a question or statement and three responses spoken in English. They will not be printed in your test book and will be spoken only one time. Select the best response to the question or statement and mark the letter (A), (B), or (C) on your answer sheet.

3. Ⓐ Ⓑ Ⓒ   5. Ⓐ Ⓑ Ⓒ   7. Ⓐ Ⓑ Ⓒ
4. Ⓐ Ⓑ Ⓒ   6. Ⓐ Ⓑ Ⓒ   8. Ⓐ Ⓑ Ⓒ

PART 3

Directions: You will hear some conversations between two or more people. You will be asked to answer three questions about what the speakers say in each conversation. Select the best response to each question and mark the letter (A), (B), (C), or (D) on your answer sheet. The conversations will not be printed in your test book and will be spoken only one time.

9. Why is the woman worried about rain?
    (A) She doesn't like rain.
    (B) She wants to do the washing.
    (C) She wants to go out.
    (D) She doesn't have a washing machine.

10. What does the weather report say about the weekend?
    (A) Saturday will be sunny.
    (B) Tomorrow is going to be rainy.
    (C) It will not rain on Sunday.
    (D) It was a nice day yesterday.

11. What will they do next?
    (A) They will check the weather report.
    (B) They will have lunch.
    (C) They will do the laundry.
    (D) They will go back to their office.

12. What is the conversation mainly about?
    (A) How to get on a ship
    (B) How to send a package
    (C) How to get a discount
    (D) How to travel to New York

13. Why does the woman say, "Sounds good"?
    (A) She is surprised.
    (B) She thinks the package is good.
    (C) She feels it is impossible.
    (D) She thinks it is a nice idea.

14. Which option did the woman choose?
    (A) Shipping by sea
    (B) Shipping by air
    (C) Shipping by both sea and rail
    (D) Shipping by rail

15. Where does the woman work?
    (A) At an airline company
    (B) At a travel agency
    (C) At a hotel
    (D) At a high school

16. What did the man probably ask the woman to do?
    (A) Look for a cheaper ticket
    (B) Find his wife and children
    (C) Read a book
    (D) Show him some tour plans

17. Where is the man going?
    (A) To Singapore
    (B) To London
    (C) To Kyoto
    (D) To Sydney

GO ON TO THE NEXT PAGE

PART 4

Directions: You will hear some talks given by a single speaker. You will be asked to answer three questions about what the speaker says in each talk. Select the best response to each question and mark the letter (A), (B), (C), or (D) on your answer sheet. The talks will not be printed in your test book and will be spoken only one time.

18. Which line had a problem?
    (A) The Blue Line
    (B) The Green Line
    (C) The Red Line
    (D) The Orange Line

19. When will the local trains most likely start running?
    (A) In a few minutes
    (B) In 10 minutes
    (C) In 30 minutes
    (D) In an hour

20. What is the cause of the delay?
    (A) An accident
    (B) The rush hour
    (C) Signal failure
    (D) The construction at the airport

21. Who most likely is Michael?
    (A) A driver
    (B) A researcher
    (C) An elderly person
    (D) A security guard

22. What kind of cars does the company want to develop?
    (A) Automatic cars
    (B) Eco-friendly cars
    (C) Cars which are kind to old people
    (D) Cars which run on diesel fuel

23. What will Michael do next?
    (A) Listen to a presentation
    (B) Make a presentation
    (C) Test a brake system
    (D) Care for elderly people

READING TEST

In the Reading test, you will read a variety of texts and answer several different types of reading comprehension questions. The entire Reading test will last 20 minutes. There are three parts, and directions are given for each part. You are encouraged to answer as many questions as possible within the time allowed.

You must mark your answers on the separate answer sheet. Do not write your answers in your test book.

PART 5

Directions: A word or phrase is missing in each of the sentences below. Four answer choices are given below each sentence. Select the best answer to complete the sentence. Then mark the letter (A), (B), (C), or (D) on your answer sheet.

24. We believe this product will be a big ------.
    (A) success
    (B) successful
    (C) succeed
    (D) successfully

    Ⓐ Ⓑ Ⓒ Ⓓ

25. This product is selling well both in America ------ in Europe.
    (A) but
    (B) and
    (C) when
    (D) that

    Ⓐ Ⓑ Ⓒ Ⓓ

26. Mike ------ sick for one week when Kaori visited his room.
    (A) is
    (B) has been
    (C) had been
    (D) will be

    Ⓐ Ⓑ Ⓒ Ⓓ

27. We must study hard ------ pass the test.
    (A) in order not to
    (B) so as not to
    (C) in spite of
    (D) so as to

    Ⓐ Ⓑ Ⓒ Ⓓ

28. We decided ------ our trip to America.
    (A) canceling
    (B) cancel
    (C) canceled
    (D) to cancel

    Ⓐ Ⓑ Ⓒ Ⓓ

29. The police are running after the ------ pickpocket.
    (A) escape
    (B) escaping
    (C) escaped
    (D) escapes

    Ⓐ Ⓑ Ⓒ Ⓓ

GO ON TO THE NEXT PAGE

30. Bill looked as if he ------- a ghost.
   (A) sees
   (B) saw
   (C) has seen
   (D) had seen

31. Johnny is a singer ------- songs are widely loved.
   (A) who
   (B) which
   (C) whose
   (D) whom

PART 6

Directions: Read the texts that follow. A word, phrase, or sentence is missing in parts of each text. Four answer choices for each question are given below the text. Select the best answer to complete the text. Then mark the letter (A), (B), (C), or (D) on your answer sheet.

Questions 32–35 refer to the following notice.

Notice to Our Guests

Please note that our swimming pool ---**32**.--- for maintenance from 5 p.m. to 6 p.m. We are also in the process of extending the reception floor for your ---**33**.---, and appreciate your patience. The swimming pool will be open regardless of the extension process except between 5 p.m. and 6 p.m. We look forward ---**34**.--- you and we hope that you will have a good time at our pool. ---**35**.---

32. (A) are closed
    (B) had been closed
    (C) closed
    (D) will be closed

33. (A) convenience
    (B) convenient
    (C) conveniently
    (D) inconvenient

34. (A) to serve
    (B) serves
    (C) serving
    (D) to serving

35. (A) The main building will be closed.
    (B) If you have any questions, please call us at 555-123-4569.
    (C) The pool had five swimming lanes.
    (D) The receptionist offered a cup of coffee.

PART 7

Directions: In this part you will read a selection of texts, such as magazine and newspaper articles, e-mails, and instant messages. Each text or set of texts is followed by several questions. Select the best answer for each question and mark the letter (A), (B), (C), or (D) on your answer sheet.

Questions 36–37 refer to the following text message chain.

Steven   9:45
Hi, what time is the sales meeting today?

Lisa   9:46
1 p.m.

Steven   9:48
Oh, sorry. I can't make it. I made an appointment with H&H Corporation for 2 p.m.

Lisa   9:49
Really? How about 11 a.m.? We need you there.

Steven   9:51
OK, that sounds good. See you then.

---

36. What is suggested about Steven's situation?
    (A) He is going to the conference room.
    (B) He has more than one appointment today.
    (C) He puts off the meeting today.
    (D) He canceled his plan.

37. At 9:48, what does Steven mean when he writes, "I can't make it"?
    (A) It's not possible for him to attend the meeting.
    (B) He can't visit H&H Corporation.
    (C) He isn't able to make a presentation.
    (D) He will see Lisa.

GO ON TO THE NEXT PAGE

Questions 38–41 refer to the following information.

Summer Rates at Star Hotels

	Weekdays Sunday–Thursday nights	Weekends Friday & Saturday nights
The Star Central Hotel	$335	$350
The Star Business Hotel	$195	$210
The Star Airport Hotel	$150	$175
The Star Resort Hotel	We offer special discounts. Please visit our website for more information! Click here	

Cancellation Policy: You may cancel your reservation for no charge until 2 days before arrival.

38. What information does the chart give?
    (A) Tour prices
    (B) Airplane fares
    (C) Hotel rates
    (D) Bus fares

39. Which hotel offers a bargain?
    (A) The Star Central Hotel
    (B) The Star Business Hotel
    (C) The Star Airport Hotel
    (D) The Star Resort Hotel

40. How can one get more information about the Star Resort Hotel?
    (A) Call the hotel
    (B) Visit their website
    (C) Get a coupon
    (D) Buy something

41. How much do guests have to pay to cancel a week before reservation?
    (A) There is no charge.
    (B) $10
    (C) $20
    (D) $30

Questions 42–45 refer to the following advertisement.

42. What kind of business is Kemal's?
    (A) A delivery company
    (B) A grocery
    (C) A bakery
    (D) A restaurant

43. For which occasion are special menus NOT served?
    (A) Birthdays
    (B) Weddings
    (C) Graduation
    (D) Anniversaries

44. When is Kemal's closed?
    (A) Monday
    (B) Thursday
    (C) Friday
    (D) Sunday

45. What should customers do if they want to book a table?
    (A) Visit a website
    (B) Fill out a form
    (C) Call the restaurant
    (D) Click a button

Questions 46–50 refer to the following schedule and e-mail.

Seminar Schedule

Date	Topic	Lecturer
Friday, Sept. 1	Marketing Your Site	Gina Harding
Saturday, Sept. 2	Site Maintenance	Tom Gaston
Sunday, Sept. 3	An Effective Website	Bob Black
Monday, Sept. 4	Trends in Internet Business	Karen Preston
Tuesday, Sept. 5	Investment in Internet Business	Luis Hunter

From: Harold Parker
To: Pauline Harvey
Date: July 20
Subject: Seminar

Dear Ms. Harvey,

I hope everything is going well with you. As you know, we are preparing for the seminar now. Unfortunately, Tom Gaston is ill and will be in the hospital in September. We are looking for a lecturer who could replace him. You are widely respected in this field, and we would be happy if you could find the time to give a lecture on September 2. Since there is not much time, I would really appreciate your reply by August 7. I look forward to hearing from you.

Regards,
Harold Parker

46. What is the main topic of this seminar?
    (A) Market research
    (B) Management proposal
    (C) Internet business
    (D) Web design

47. What is the main purpose of the e-mail?
    (A) To thank Pauline for her help
    (B) To ask Pauline for help
    (C) To cancel a seminar
    (D) To give a greeting

48. What does Harold ask Pauline to do?
    (A) Give him a reply
    (B) Thank him
    (C) Visit him
    (D) Go for a drink with him

49. What is suggested about Tom Gaston?
    (A) He has written a book.
    (B) He has canceled a lecture.
    (C) He has worked in the hospital.
    (D) He has refused to do maintenance.

50. What day does Harold Parker need a lecturer?
    (A) Friday
    (B) Saturday
    (C) Sunday
    (D) Monday

GO ON TO THE NEXT PAGE

Unit 1 Daily Life
名詞と代名詞

Vocabulary

1 1～20の語句を聞き取り、下の枠内から選んでA欄に書きましょう。

breakfast	brush	carry	climb	daily life
do the laundry	e-mail address	garden	hang	hobby
information	lean	location	move in	part-time job
rent	sweep	teeth	wake up	water

🎧 02   A   B

1. _____ _____
2. _____ _____
3. _____ _____
4. _____ _____
5. _____ _____
6. _____ _____
7. _____ _____
8. _____ _____
9. _____ _____
10. _____ _____

🎧 03   A   B

11. _____ _____
12. _____ _____
13. _____ _____
14. _____ _____
15. _____ _____
16. _____ _____
17. _____ _____
18. _____ _____
19. _____ _____
20. _____ _____

2 もう一度音声を聞き、1～20の語句の意味を下の枠内から選んでB欄に書きましょう。

アルバイト	eメールアドレス	掛ける	趣味	情報
洗濯する	朝食	賃貸料	日常生活	庭
登る	歯	掃く	運ぶ	場所
引っ越してくる	磨く	水をやる	目が覚める	もたれる

Listening Section

Key Point [Part 1] 進行形(be 動詞 + doing)の表現に慣れよう!

Part 1では、「○○が〜しているところです」と人物の動作を表す進行形が多く使用されます。

He **is brushing** his teeth. (彼は歯を磨いている。)
A man **is leaning** against a wall. (男性が壁にもたれかかっている。)
The woman **is typing**. (その女性はタイピングしている。)
A man **is carrying** books. (男性が本を運んでいる。)
They **are climbing** a ladder. (彼らははしごを登っている。)
The woman **is doing** the laundry. (その女性は洗濯をしている。)
The men **are sweeping** the floor. (その男性たちが床を掃いている。)

Try 1　次のタスクに取り組みましょう。

1 音声を聞いて、右の写真の様子を最もよく表している
英文を (A) 〜 (C) より1つ選びましょう。　🎧 04

Ⓐ　Ⓑ　Ⓒ

2 もう一度音声を聞き、＿＿部分を埋めましょう。そして、1の答えを確認しましょう。　🎧 04

(A) They ＿＿＿＿ ＿＿＿＿ ＿＿＿＿ ＿＿＿＿.

(B) The men and women ＿＿＿＿ ＿＿＿＿.

(C) They are ＿＿＿＿ ＿＿＿＿ the wall.

Try 2　音声を聞き、＿＿部分を埋めましょう。　🎧 05

1. She ＿＿＿＿ ＿＿＿＿ the ＿＿＿＿ in the ＿＿＿＿.
2. People ＿＿＿＿ ＿＿＿＿ in front of the ＿＿＿＿.
3. They ＿＿＿＿ ＿＿＿＿ ＿＿＿＿ ＿＿＿＿ on the ＿＿＿＿.
4. They ＿＿＿＿ ＿＿＿＿ ＿＿＿＿ ＿＿＿＿.

Try 3

音声を聞いて、それぞれの写真の様子を最もよく表している英文を選びましょう。

06-07

1.

Ⓐ Ⓑ Ⓒ Ⓓ

2.

Ⓐ Ⓑ Ⓒ Ⓓ

Active Reading 08

目標：＿＿秒　1回目：＿＿秒　2回目：＿＿秒

Breakfast

A lot of people skip breakfast to lose weight and become healthier, but there's research that breakfast is the most important meal of the day. On average, people who eat breakfast have better diets than those who don't. Breakfast eaters are also less likely to have heart disease, and are more physically and mentally active. Breakfast has an effect on you that's different from any other meal, because people spend a long time not eating between the time they sleep and wake up. What we eat during breakfast is also important, so try to have something good for breakfast.

語注　skip 抜かす　lose weight やせる　on average 概して　diet 飲食物　physically 肉体的に　mentally 精神的に

◆ 以下が上の文章に合っていればT、間違っていればFを [ ] に書きましょう。Fの場合は訂正しましょう。

1. [　] 朝食は一日で最も大切な食事であるという研究がある。

2. [　] 朝食を食べる人は心臓病になりにくい。

Reading Section

Key Point [Part 5 & 6] 品詞1：名詞と代名詞

[名詞] 人 (Tom) や物 (desk)、概念 (happiness) などの名称を示すものです。

名詞によくつく接尾辞

-ness	happi**ness**, sad**ness**, ill**ness**, polite**ness**
-sion / -tion	deci**sion**, inclu**sion**, introduc**tion**, educa**tion**, motiva**tion**
-ment	judg**ment**, disappoint**ment**, move**ment**, pay**ment**

[人称代名詞] 用法によって形 (格) が変わります。Try 1の表を完成させましょう。

Try 1　下の表を完成させましょう。（解答は巻末のAppendixに掲載しています。）

人称代名詞の変化表

単数形／複数形	主格（〜は／が）	所有格（〜の）	目的格（〜を／に）	所有代名詞（〜のもの）	再帰代名詞（〜自身）
私	I				
私たち			us		
あなた		your			
あなたたち					
彼				his	
彼ら					
彼女					herself
彼女たち					
それ				—	
それら					

Try 2　次の英文の空所に入る最も適切な語句を選びましょう。

If you would like further information, please visit ------- website at www.save.com.

(A) we
(B) our
(C) us
(D) ours

HINT "------- website" で「私たちのウェブサイト」という意味になるものはどれでしょうか。

（訳）もっと詳しい情報をご希望でしたら、私たちのウェブサイト、www.save.comをご覧ください。

Think / Write / Share

ペアまたはグループで協力してやりましょう。

A 一人は前のページの代名詞の表を見て、もう一人はテキストを閉じます。互いに代名詞の問題を出して、答えてみましょう。

(例)

B メンバーの名前を尋ね、その回答を書きましょう。質問された人はIやmyで始まる自己紹介文を言ってみましょう。

A: What's your name?

B: (例) *I am Takeshi. My hobby is listening to music.*

C メンバーに兄弟・姉妹について尋ね、その回答を書きましょう。

A: Do you have any brothers or sisters?

B: (例) *Yes, I have a brother.*

A: What's his/her name? How old is he/she?

B: (例) *His name is Takeru. He is 17.*

D メンバーにアルバイトについて尋ね、その回答を書きましょう。

A: Do you have a part-time job?

B: (例) *Yes, I work at a café. Our café is near the university.*

E 下の単語の中から5つの名詞を丸で囲みましょう。また、見つけた名詞の共通点を書きましょう。

introduction	locate	inform	add	satisfaction
location	introduce	addition	satisfy	information

共通点:(　　　　　　　　　　　　　　　　　　　　　　　　　　　　)

Try 3 英文の空所に入る最も適切な語句を選びましょう。

1. Nick usually cooks for -------.
   (A) he
   (B) his
   (C) himself

2. I received a good -------.
   (A) educate
   (B) educational
   (C) education

3. She is the author of a bestselling novel and ------ title is *Harry Potter*.
   (A) his
   (B) it
   (C) its

4. You should be careful about when ------- rent is due.
   (A) you
   (B) your
   (C) yours

5. I asked ------- his e-mail address.
   (A) her
   (B) she
   (C) hers

6. My mother showed her ------- because of my test result.
   (A) disappoints
   (B) disappointment
   (C) disappoint

Try 4 英文の空所に入る最も適切な語句を選びましょう。

1. My home is in a good ------- for commuting.
   (A) location
   (B) located
   (C) locating
   (D) locates

2. It's ------- turn to water the flowers.
   (A) theirs
   (B) yours
   (C) your
   (D) they

3. She received the present from -------.
   (A) he
   (B) his
   (C) him
   (D) they

4. Since I moved in last month, I have needed more ------- about daily life here.
   (A) inform
   (B) informs
   (C) information
   (D) informing

Unit 2 Health

動詞・形容詞・副詞

Vocabulary

1 1〜20の語句を聞き取り、下の枠内から選んでA欄に書きましょう。

cold	cure	disease	exercise	fever
gym	headache	health	hospital	lose weight
medicine	patient	quit	recover	runny nose
see a doctor	smoking	stomachache	strong	tired

🎧 09   A   B
1. _____ _____
2. _____ _____
3. _____ _____
4. _____ _____
5. _____ _____
6. _____ _____
7. _____ _____
8. _____ _____
9. _____ _____
10. _____ _____

🎧 10   A   B
11. _____ _____
12. _____ _____
13. _____ _____
14. _____ _____
15. _____ _____
16. _____ _____
17. _____ _____
18. _____ _____
19. _____ _____
20. _____ _____

2 もう一度音声を聞き、1〜20の語句の意味を下の枠内から選んでB欄に書きましょう。

医者に診てもらう	胃痛	運動する	回復する	風邪
患者	薬	健康	ジム	頭痛
タバコを吸うこと	疲れた	強い	治す	熱
鼻水	病院	病気	やせる	やめる

Listening Section

Key Point [Part 2] 疑問文への答え方に慣れよう！

WH疑問文のときの応答パターン：疑問詞に応じた具体的な内容で答える

When did you quit smoking?——On April 1.
（いつタバコを吸うのをやめましたか。——4月1日です。）

How did you cure your cold?——By just sleeping.
（どうやって風邪を治しましたか。——ただ眠って治しました。）

WH疑問文以外の疑問文への応答パターン：Yes/Noや具体的な内容で答える

Do you know which medicine is good for a headache?——Yes, this one is good.
（どの薬が頭痛に効くか知っていますか。——はい、これが効きます。）

Are you going to see a doctor today?——No, tomorrow.
（今日、病院に行くつもりですか。——いいえ、明日です。）

Do you have a fever?——It's 38.5 degrees. （熱がありますか。——38.5度です。）

WH疑問文で使われる疑問詞

When ...?「いつ」（時間や日程など）	Where ...?「どこ」（場所）
What ...?「何を、何が」（物事や出来事など）	Who ...?「誰」（人）
Why ...?「なぜ」（理由）	How ...?「どのように」（方法や経緯など）
How often ...?「どれくらいの頻度で」（頻度や回数）	How many ...?「いくつ」（数）
How long ...?「どれくらい」（時間や期間・日数など）	How much ...?「どれくらい」（量）
How far ...?「どれくらい」（距離）	How old ...?「何歳」（年齢）

Try 1 次のタスクに取り組みましょう。

1 音声を聞いて、質問文に対する最も適切な応答文を (A) 〜 (C) から選びましょう。 🎧 11

Ⓐ　Ⓑ　Ⓒ

2 もう一度音声を聞き、＿＿部分を埋めましょう。そして、1 の答えを確認しましょう。 🎧 11

＿＿＿＿＿＿ often do you go to the ＿＿＿＿＿＿?

(A) ＿＿＿＿＿＿, I went there ＿＿＿＿＿＿.

(B) ＿＿＿＿＿＿ a week.

(C) ＿＿＿＿＿＿, I ＿＿＿＿＿＿ ＿＿＿＿＿＿.

Try 2

音声を聞き、____部分を埋めましょう。 🎧 12

1. _____ _____ to the _____?

   —— My _____ did because she had a bad _____.

2. _____ _____ _____ _____ for your _____?

   —— I _____ _____ _____.

3. What kind of symptoms do you have?

   —— I have a _____ _____ _____ _____ _____.

4. _____ _____ _____ so _____?

   —— I _____ _____ _____ every night.

5. _____ is the _____ _____?

   —— _____ _____.

Try 3

音声を聞いて、質問文に対する最も適切な応答文を (A) 〜 (C) から選びましょう。 🎧 13-15

1. Ⓐ Ⓑ Ⓒ   2. Ⓐ Ⓑ Ⓒ   3. Ⓐ Ⓑ Ⓒ

Active Reading 🎧 16

目標：____秒　1回目：____秒　2回目：____秒

How Technology Is Changing Health Care

A lot of money is being spent recently on improving technology that helps keep people healthy. Researchers at IBM are using the same technology they use for "Watson." Watson is a clever computer that beat two former champions of the quiz game show *Jeopardy*. Watson is used to help doctors keep patient records and diagnose illnesses faster. There are various activity trackers on the market today. They look like watches and bracelets and help people keep a record of their exercise, diet, and sleep. Hopefully, these technologies will continue to help all of us stay healthier and live longer.

語注　improve 向上させる　clever 賢い　beat 打ち負かす　record 記録　diagnose 診断する　continue 続く

◆ 上の文章に関する質問に日本語で答えましょう。

1. Watson とは何ですか。 _____

2. activity tracker というものは、どのような形状で何をするものですか。

_____

Reading Section

Key Point [Part 5 & 6] 品詞2：動詞・形容詞・副詞

[動詞] 動作や状態を表します。
　　Our teacher **teaches** English. （私たちの先生は英語を教える。）

[形容詞] 主語の状態を表したり、名詞を修飾したりします。
　　Our **English** teacher is **great**. （私たちの英語の先生はすばらしい。）

[副詞] 動詞・形容詞・副詞を修飾する
　　The great English teacher teaches English **kindly**. （そのすばらしい英語の先生は英語を親切に教える。）

名詞	information	「情報」	He collects the **information** of his disease. （彼は自分の病気の情報を集めている。）
動詞	inform	「知らせる」	The doctor **informed** him of his condition. （医者は彼に自分の体調について知らせた。）
形容詞	informative	「有益な」	He got **informative** advice. （彼は有益な助言を得た。）
副詞	informatively	「有益に」	He uses it **informatively**. （彼は有益にそれを用いている。）

それぞれの品詞によくつく接尾辞

動詞	-ize	apolog**ize**, critic**ize**, hospital**ize**
	-fy	satis**fy**, clari**fy**, simpli**fy**
形容詞	-ful	beauti**ful**, care**ful**, use**ful**
	-y	funn**y**, rain**y**, sleep**y**, ic**y**
	-ive	effect**ive**, posit**ive**, expens**ive**
副詞	-ly	happi**ly**, beautiful**ly**, final**ly**

Try 1 次の英文の空所に入る最も適切な語を選びましょう。

The doctor examined the patient -------.
(A) care　　(B) careful　　(C) carefully　　(D) caring

HINT 空所に入る語はexaminedという動詞を修飾しています。
（訳）その医者は患者を注意深く診察した。

Think / Write / Share

ペアまたはグループで協力してやりましょう。

A 下線部の品詞は何でしょうか。

1. We are waiting for an <u>active</u> remedy for the disease.　　　(　　　　　)
   私たちはその病気の<u>即効性のある</u>薬を待っている。

2. Her ability to take <u>action</u> is wonderful.　　　(　　　　　)
   彼女の<u>行動</u>力はすばらしい。

3. The medicine is being <u>actively</u> researched.　　　(　　　　　)
   その薬は<u>盛んに</u>研究されている。

4. The heart <u>acts</u> as a pump.　　　(　　　　　)
   心臓はポンプの<u>働きをする</u>。

B 下の20の単語を名詞・動詞・形容詞・副詞に分類しましょう。ただし、2つに当てはまるものもいくつかあります。

| carefully   easily   care   strong   clean   strength   beautifully   easy |
| careful   additional   clear   strongly   powerful   beauty   strengthen |
| powerfully   add   addition   ease   additionally   clearly   power   beautiful |

名詞：＿＿＿＿＿＿＿＿＿＿＿＿＿＿＿＿＿＿＿＿＿＿＿＿＿＿＿＿＿＿

動詞：＿＿＿＿＿＿＿＿＿＿＿＿＿＿＿＿＿＿＿＿＿＿＿＿＿＿＿＿＿＿

形容詞：＿＿＿＿＿＿＿＿＿＿＿＿＿＿＿＿＿＿＿＿＿＿＿＿＿＿＿＿

副詞：＿＿＿＿＿＿＿＿＿＿＿＿＿＿＿＿＿＿＿＿＿＿＿＿＿＿＿＿＿＿

C 例にならって書き換えましょう。

（例）Suzy is a powerful singer. →　Suzy sings powerfully.

1. He is a careful researcher. → ＿＿＿＿＿＿＿＿＿＿＿＿＿＿＿＿＿

2. You are a slow speaker. → ＿＿＿＿＿＿＿＿＿＿＿＿＿＿＿＿＿＿

3. Mark is an active worker. → ＿＿＿＿＿＿＿＿＿＿＿＿＿＿＿＿＿

Try 2 次の英文の空所に入る最も適切な語句を選びましょう。

1. Sports ------- our bodies and minds.
   (A) strong
   (B) strength
   (C) strengthen

2. He was sick last month and now he is ------- recovering.
   (A) slower
   (B) slowly
   (C) slowness

3. Bill got tired after even ------- exercises.
   (A) ease
   (B) easily
   (C) easy

4. The doctor made a ------- to move him to a larger hospital.
   (A) decision
   (B) decisive
   (C) decide

Try 3 文章の4つの空所に入る最も適切な語句または文をそれぞれ選びましょう。

If you want to ---1.--- in getting in shape, you should try our gym!

This gym is very ---2.--- because it's near the station. You can exercise on your way home.

Everyone loses weight ---3.---, so you can go at your own pace. ---4.---

1. (A) successfully
   (B) success
   (C) succeed
   (D) successful

2. (A) convenience
   (B) conveniently
   (C) convenient
   (D) inconvenient

3. (A) differ
   (B) difference
   (C) different
   (D) differently

4. (A) For more information, please call 555-1111 or visit www.goodshape.com.
   (B) Entrance to the fair is $5 for adults and $2 for children.
   (C) The gym is only 3 minutes from the station!
   (D) The staff you work with will check your performance.

Unit 3 Education

時制1

Vocabulary

1 1〜20の語句を聞き取り、下の枠内から選んでA欄に書きましょう。

absence	attend	belong to	cancel	circle
class	conversation	deadline	do one's best	dormitory
grade	homework	library	major	professor
school cafeteria	subject	submit	take place	university

🎧 17　　A　　　　　B　　　　　🎧 18　　A　　　　　B

1. _____ _____　　11. _____ _____
2. _____ _____　　12. _____ _____
3. _____ _____　　13. _____ _____
4. _____ _____　　14. _____ _____
5. _____ _____　　15. _____ _____
6. _____ _____　　16. _____ _____
7. _____ _____　　17. _____ _____
8. _____ _____　　18. _____ _____
9. _____ _____　　19. _____ _____
10. _____ _____　　20. _____ _____

2 もう一度音声を聞き、1〜20の語句の意味を下の枠内から選んでB欄に書きましょう。

行われる	会話	学食	休講にする	教科
教授	欠席	最善を尽くす	サークル	締切
授業	宿題	出席する	成績	専攻
大学	提出する	図書館	〜に所属する	寮

Listening Section

🔑 Key Point [Part 3] 設問のポイントをすばやく押さえてから聞こう！

会話の内容をすべて記憶しながら聞くのは簡単ではありません。Part 3 では先に設問に目を通して、聞き取るべきポイントを把握してから会話を聞く必要があります。

3つの設問の ◯ で囲んである語句がポイントです。疑問詞は必ず押さえましょう。

1. [Where] is this [conversation] [taking place]?　　1. どこで、会話、行う
   (A) ...
   (B) ...
2. [Why] is the [man] in a [hurry]?　　2. なぜ、男性、急いでいる
   (A) ...
   (B) ...
3. [Where] will the [man] [go] [next]?　　3. どこに、男性、行く、次に
   (A) ...
   (B) ...

🔊 Try 1　次のタスクに取り組みましょう。

[1] 以下の2つの設問の ◯ で囲んだ語句を見て、聞き取りポイントをまとめましょう。

　1. [When] is the [deadline] for the [report]?　　_____

　2. [Where] is this [conversation] [taking place]?　_____

[2] 2人の会話を聞き、[1] の各設問の答えとして最も適切なものを選びましょう。　🎧 19

　1. (A) Today　　　　　　　　　　　**2.** (A) At a school cafeteria
　　(B) On May 12　　　　　　　　　　　(B) On a train
　　(C) On May 16　　　　　　　　　　　(C) In the man's house

[3] もう一度会話を聞き、____部分を埋めましょう。そして、[2] の答えを確認しましょう。　🎧 19

　W: Gee ... I have to _____ _____ _____ for the _____

　　_____.

　M: I've already _____ them. It's _____ _____ today.

　　_____ _____ _____.

　W: OK. I'll do my best. Can I call you if I have any _____?

　M: Sure. Oh, I'm _____ at my _____. I'll see you later. Bye.

Try 2 音声を聞き、____部分を埋めましょう。 🎧 20

1. _____ did you _____ the _____?
2. _____ _____ _____ you do the _____?
3. _____ is the _____ for _____ _____?
4. _____ _____ the _____ of the _____?

Try 3 2人の会話を聞き、設問の答えとして最も適切なものを選びましょう。 🎧 21

1. Why does the woman want to be helped?
   (A) To finish her English homework
   (B) To do her math homework
   (C) To go to the library
   (D) To go to her part-time job
   Ⓐ Ⓑ Ⓒ Ⓓ

2. When will they meet again?
   (A) On Monday
   (B) This afternoon
   (C) This evening
   (D) Tomorrow afternoon
   Ⓐ Ⓑ Ⓒ Ⓓ

3. Where will they study?
   (A) In a school library
   (B) In a classroom
   (C) At John's house
   (D) At the school cafeteria
   Ⓐ Ⓑ Ⓒ Ⓓ

Active Reading 🎧 22

目標：____秒　1回目：____秒　2回目：____秒

Life as a Student Around the Globe

Katherine Burch interviewed three students from different countries about student life where they are from, and here is what the students said. See how your school life compares to theirs.

		Turkey	USA	Norway
Studying	Hours Per Week	10 to 20	40	8 to 10
	Lectures Per Week	10 to 13 hours	4 to 5 hours	3 to 6 hours
	Student Age Range	18 to 30	18 to 30	19 to 70
Fun	Activities	spending time with friends, going to clubs, bars and restaurants	going out to movies, swing dancing, volunteering	skiing, football, working part-time, hanging out

上の説明と表に合うように、以下の空所を国名（カタカナ）で埋めましょう。

1. 学校に高齢の学生がいると答えたのは（　　　　　　）の学生。
2. 楽しみの一つとしてボランティア活動を挙げたのは（　　　　　　　）の学生。

Reading Section

🔑 Key Point ［Part 5 & 6］ 時制（基本時制・進行形）

時制は次の12種類あります。

基本時制	現在	過去	未来
進行形	現在進行形 am/is/are + *doing*	過去進行形 was/were + *doing*	未来進行形 will be + *doing*
完了形	現在完了 have/has + 過去分詞	過去完了（大過去） had + 過去分詞	未来完了 will have + 過去分詞
完了進行形	現在完了進行形 have been + *doing*	過去完了進行形 had been + *doing*	未来完了進行形 will have been + *doing*

現在時制	Keiko **has** a boyfriend. （ケイコには彼がいる。）
過去時制	Keiko **had** a boyfriend. （ケイコには彼がいた。）
未来時制	Keiko **will have** a boyfriend. （ケイコには彼ができるだろう。）
現在進行形	Ken **is going** out with his girlfriend. （ケンは彼女とデートしている。）
過去進行形	Ken **was going** out with his girlfriend. （ケンは彼女とデートしていた。）
未来進行形	Ken **will be going** out with his girlfriend. （ケンは彼女とデートしているだろう。）

ふつう進行形にしない動詞：もともとの意味に進行形の意味合いを含んでいます。

belong「属している」	exist「存在する」	know「知っている」
possess「持っている」	remain「〜のままである」	resemble「似ている」

📖 Try 1　次の英文の空所に入る最も適切な語句を選びましょう。

She ------- her teacher yesterday about the test.

(A) asks
(B) asked
(C) will ask
(D) asking

HINT　yesterdayから時制を考えましょう。
（訳）彼女は昨日、テストについて先生に尋ねた。

Think / Write / Share

ペアまたはグループで協力してやりましょう。

A メンバーの学年・学部・クラブ / サークルを尋ね、その回答を書きましょう。今の状態やいつもしていることを述べる場合は現在時制の文を使います。

1. A: What year are you in?
   B: (例) I'm a <u>freshman</u>. (sophomore / junior / senior)

   _____

2. A: What's your major?
   B: (例) My major is <u>commerce</u>. (economics / literature / law / engineering / music)

   _____

3. A: Do you belong to any clubs or circles?
   B: (例) I belong to the <u>baseball club</u>. (tennis circle / music club)

   _____

B メンバーに中学・高校のときの部活動についても尋ね、その回答を書きましょう。過去のことを述べる場合は過去時制の文を使います。

1. A: Did you belong to any clubs or circles when you were a junior high school student?
   B: (例) I belonged to the baseball club. / No, I didn't.

   _____

2. A: Did you belong to any clubs or circles when you were a high school student?
   B: (例) I belonged to the <u>baseball club</u>. (basketball club / ESS club)

   _____

C メンバーに夏休みの計画について尋ね、その回答を書きましょう。未来のことを述べる場合は未来時制の文を使います。

A: What are you going to do during summer vacation?
B: (例) I'm going to go to America.

_____

Try 2 次の英文の空所に入る最も適切な語句を選びましょう。

1. Peter ------- to a school camp in California next summer.
   (A) go
   (B) went
   (C) will go
   Ⓐ Ⓑ Ⓒ

2. Professor Jackson ------- his class because he had a cold.
   (A) cancel
   (B) canceled
   (C) canceling
   Ⓐ Ⓑ Ⓒ

3. A lot of students ------- in the school cafeteria.
   (A) eat
   (B) eating
   (C) eats
   Ⓐ Ⓑ Ⓒ

4. Be quiet. I'm ------- for the exam now.
   (A) study
   (B) studied
   (C) studying
   Ⓐ Ⓑ Ⓒ

5. Kate ------- the class at this time tomorrow.
   (A) taking
   (B) was taking
   (C) will be taking
   Ⓐ Ⓑ Ⓒ

6. He ------- soccer when I saw him yesterday.
   (A) is playing
   (B) was playing
   (C) will be playing
   Ⓐ Ⓑ Ⓒ

Try 3 英文の空所に入る最も適切な語句を選びましょう。

1. My vacation ------- over in a week.
   (A) be
   (B) are
   (C) been
   (D) will be
   Ⓐ Ⓑ Ⓒ Ⓓ

2. Gerry ------- her class and got a good grade.
   (A) attend
   (B) attending
   (C) attended
   (D) will attend
   Ⓐ Ⓑ Ⓒ Ⓓ

3. They ------- the biology club.
   (A) belong
   (B) belong to
   (C) belonging to
   (D) were belonging
   Ⓐ Ⓑ Ⓒ Ⓓ

4. I ------- Kanae's book to her last week.
   (A) return
   (B) returns
   (C) returned
   (D) will return
   Ⓐ Ⓑ Ⓒ Ⓓ

Unit 4 Travel

時制 2

Vocabulary

1 1〜20の語句を聞き取り、下の枠内から選んでA欄に書きましょう。

accommodations	book	brochure	buffet	cellphone
check in	concierge	counter	exchange	hospitality
hotel	itinerary	luggage	pay-phone	reception desk
restroom	souvenir	tour guide	tourist	travel agency

🎧 23　　A　　　　　B　　　　　　🎧 24　　A　　　　　B

1. _____ _____   11. _____ _____
2. _____ _____   12. _____ _____
3. _____ _____   13. _____ _____
4. _____ _____   14. _____ _____
5. _____ _____   15. _____ _____
6. _____ _____   16. _____ _____
7. _____ _____   17. _____ _____
8. _____ _____   18. _____ _____
9. _____ _____   19. _____ _____
10. _____ _____   20. _____ _____

2 もう一度音声を聞き、1〜20の語句の意味を下の枠内から選んでB欄に書きましょう。

受付	おみやげ	おもてなし	カウンター	観光客
携帯電話	交換する	公衆電話	コンシェルジュ	宿泊設備
食堂	チェックインする	ツアーガイド	手荷物	トイレ
パンフレット	ホテル	予約する	旅行代理店	旅程表

Listening Section

🔑 Key Point ［Part 1］ 位置関係を示す表現をマスターしよう！

Part 1の写真描写問題では、人や物の位置関係を示す表現が多く使われます。次の例文では、◯と□で囲んだ人・物の位置関係が■で囲んだ語句で表されています。

(Two brochures) have been placed **on** the [table]. （2枚のパンフレットがテーブルの上に置かれている。）
(A money exchange booth) is **next to** the [concierge]. （両替ブースはコンシェルジュの隣にある。）
(A picture) is hanging **on** the [wall]. （絵が壁に掛かっている。）
(A few tourists) are waiting **in front of** the [hotel]. （2、3人の観光客がホテルの前で待っている。）

位置関係でよく使われる語句：

above ～「(離れて)～の上に」	across from ～「～の対面に」	against ～「～にもたれて［接して］」
at ～「～に」	behind ～「～の後ろに」	between A and B「A と B の間に」
in ～「～の中に」	in front of ～「～の前に」	near / by ～「～の近くに」
next to ～「～の隣に」	on ～「(くっついて)～の上に」	under ～「～の下に」

🔊 Try 1   次のタスクに取り組みましょう。

[1] 音声を聞いて、右の写真の様子を最もよく表しているものを (A) ～ (C) より1つ選びましょう。 🎧 25

Ⓐ　Ⓑ　Ⓒ

[2] もう一度音声を聞き、___部分を埋めましょう。そして、[1]の答えを確認しましょう。 🎧 25

(A) There is a _____ _____ the _____ _____.

(B) Some _____ have been placed _____ _____ the _____.

(C) The _____ is _____ the _____.

40　Unit 4　Travel　時制 2

Try 2

音声を聞き、____部分を埋めましょう。 🎧 26

1. The _____ is _____ the _____.
2. The _____ _____ is _____ _____ the hotel.
3. A _____ and _____ _____ are on the _____.
4. The _____ is _____ the _____ and the _____ _____.

Try 3

音声を聞いて、それぞれの写真の様子を最もよく表している英文を選びましょう。 🎧 27-28

1.

Ⓐ Ⓑ Ⓒ Ⓓ

2.

Ⓐ Ⓑ Ⓒ Ⓓ

Active Reading 🎧 29

目標：____秒　1回目：____秒　2回目：____秒

Strange New Year's Traditions

Most countries celebrate New Year's on the same day and at the same time every year, but there are some strange ways to celebrate it. In South Africa, people throw out old appliances and furniture from their verandas, sometimes even large ones like refrigerators and sofas. Some men from Scotland walk around swinging balls of fire on poles over their heads to remove bad things from the coming year. In the Philippines, people believe that round shapes bring prosperity, so they buy round fruits and wear clothes with polka dots to welcome New Year's. There are many more unusual New Year's traditions in every country. Do you know of any others?

語注　celebrate 祝う　appliance 家電製品　furniture 家具　refrigerator 冷蔵庫　prosperity 繁栄　polka dot 水玉模様

◆ 以下が上の文章に合っていればT、間違っていればFを[ ]に書きましょう。Fの場合は訂正しましょう。

1. [ ] 新年を祝うために、ベランダから冷蔵庫やソファを投げるのは南アフリカの人である。
2. [ ] フィリピンの人は四角い物が繁栄をもたらすと考えている。

Reading Section

Key Point [Part 5 & 6] 完了形

完了形には次の3種類があり、すべてに共通するポイントは時間に幅があることです。したがって、時間の一点を指す語句や表現（yesterday や on the 5th など）とは一緒に使えません。

現在完了形	have/has ＋過去分詞
過去完了形	had ＋過去分詞
未来完了形	will have ＋過去分詞

現在完了形：過去からの出来事が現在に影響を及ぼしています。

- 完了　I **have seen** off my aunt at the airport.（叔母を見送りに空港へ行ってきたところだ。）
- 結果　My brother **has gone** to Hokkaido.（私の兄は北海道へ行った［今はいない］。）
- 経験　**Have** you ever **been** to Hawaii?（今までにハワイへ行ったことがありますか。）
- 継続　He **has been** sleeping on the train.（彼は列車の中で眠り続けている。）

→継続の用法は通例、完了進行形（have/has または had been *doing*）をとります。ただし、「進行形にしない動詞」は、もともと同じ状態が続くことを表すので、完了進行形は使いません。

She **has known** that hotel since she was a child.
（彼女は子供の頃からあのホテルを知っている。）

p. 36を見よう

時制のまとめ

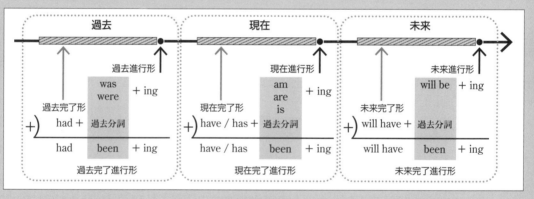

Try 1　次の英文の空所に入る最も適切な語句を選びましょう。

He ------- Rome once before.

(A) will visit　　(B) visit　　(C) visiting　　(D) has visited

HINT　once before（以前に一度）から、経験を述べていることがわかります。
（訳）彼は以前に一度ローマを訪れたことがある。

Think / Write / Share

ペアまたはグループで協力してやりましょう。

A 以下の文を訳し、疑問文にしてみましょう。疑問文にするときは、主語を you にしましょう。

1. I have been to Hawaii.
   訳：(　　　　　　　　　　　　　　　　　　　　　　　　　　　　　　)
   疑問文：_____

2. I have lost my cellphone twice.
   訳：(　　　　　　　　　　　　　　　　　　　　　　　　　　　　　　)
   疑問文：_____

3. I have been busy since morning.
   訳：(　　　　　　　　　　　　　　　　　　　　　　　　　　　　　　)
   疑問文：_____

4. I have had a snack.
   訳：(　　　　　　　　　　　　　　　　　　　　　　　　　　　　　　)
   疑問文：_____

B 上で作った疑問文を使って、クラスのみんなに質問し、次の空所にクラスメイトの名前を入れましょう。

_____ has been to Hawaii.

_____ has lost his/her cellphone twice.

_____ has been busy since morning.

_____ has had a snack.

Try 2　英文の空所に入る最も適切な語句を選びましょう。

1. He has recently ------- from London.
   (A) return
   (B) returned
   (C) returns
   　Ⓐ Ⓑ Ⓒ

2. Rogers has already ------- his flight.
   (A) booked
   (B) book
   (C) booking
   　Ⓐ Ⓑ Ⓒ

3. ------- you exchanged your yen for dollars yet?
   (A) Do
   (B) Have
   (C) Has
   　Ⓐ Ⓑ Ⓒ

4. That travel agency has never ------- us with their service.
   (A) disappointed
   (B) disappoint
   (C) disappoints
   　Ⓐ Ⓑ Ⓒ

5. I ------- to a Japanese garden like this in Australia.
   (A) has
   (B) had been
   (C) have been
   Ⓐ Ⓑ Ⓒ

6. Jack ------- never had sushi until he came to Japan.
   (A) have
   (B) had
   (C) has
   Ⓐ Ⓑ Ⓒ

7. The tour guide ------- for the guests at the lobby since 7 a.m.
   (A) waiting
   (B) been waiting
   (C) has been waiting
   Ⓐ Ⓑ Ⓒ

8. He ------- back home by next Sunday.
   (A) had come
   (B) will have come
   (C) have come
   Ⓐ Ⓑ Ⓒ

Try 3 文章の4つの空所に入る最も適切な語句または文をそれぞれ選びましょう。

Dear Jenny,

I had never ---**1**.--- Kinkakuji before, but I had been wanting to do so. ---**2**.--- I'm still excited though it ---**3**.--- since I got to Kyoto.

I checked in at the hotel after visiting Kinkakuji. The hotel is very big and has accommodations for 300 guests. Japanese hospitality is excellent! The restaurant in the hotel I reserved for lunch ---**4**.--- for me even though I arrived late.

I took a lot of pictures. I'm looking forward to showing them to you.

Love,
Mary

1. (A) visiting
   (B) visit
   (C) visited
   (D) visits
   Ⓐ Ⓑ Ⓒ Ⓓ

2. (A) I will get to the hotel by train.
   (B) At last, I went there today.
   (C) I have seen you three times.
   (D) I hope to visit there again.
   Ⓐ Ⓑ Ⓒ Ⓓ

3. (A) has raining
   (B) has been raining
   (C) has been rained
   (D) had raining
   Ⓐ Ⓑ Ⓒ Ⓓ

4. (A) wait
   (B) waiting
   (C) have waiting
   (D) had been waiting
   Ⓐ Ⓑ Ⓒ Ⓓ

Unit 5 Transportation

前置詞

Vocabulary

1 1〜20の語句を聞き取り、下の枠内から選んでA欄に書きましょう。

aisle seat	arrival time	be bound for	change trains	commuter pass
delay	departure time	destination	fare	lost and found
on time	parking lot	passenger	reserve	station
subway	take a taxi	transportation	trip	window seat

🎧 30   A   B

1. _____ _____
2. _____ _____
3. _____ _____
4. _____ _____
5. _____ _____
6. _____ _____
7. _____ _____
8. _____ _____
9. _____ _____
10. _____ _____

🎧 31   A   B

11. _____ _____
12. _____ _____
13. _____ _____
14. _____ _____
15. _____ _____
16. _____ _____
17. _____ _____
18. _____ _____
19. _____ _____
20. _____ _____

2 もう一度音声を聞き、1〜20の語句の意味を下の枠内から選んでB欄に書きましょう。

〜行きである	遺失物取扱所	運賃	駅	遅らせる
交通機関	時間通りに	出発時刻	乗客	タクシーに乗る
地下鉄	駐車場	通路側の席	定期券	電車を乗り換える
到着時刻	窓側の席	目的地	旅行	予約する

Listening Section

Key Point ［Part 2］ 提案・依頼・許可への応答パターンに慣れよう！

会話には広く一般的に用いられる決まったパターンがあり、Part 2でもよく見受けられます。特に、提案・依頼・許可を表す質問文は頻出です。

●提案する「〜しませんか」「〜してはどうですか」

Why don't we take the next bus?——Why not?（次のバスに乗りませんか。——もちろんです。）
▷他の提案の表現　Why don't you 〜?「〜してはどうですか」　How about 〜?「〜はどうですか」
　　　　　　　　Let's 〜.「〜しましょう」　Shall we 〜?「（一緒に）〜しませんか」
▷応答パターン　承諾　Sounds good.「いいですね」
　　　　　　　　断り　I'm sorry, but ...「すみませんが…」
　　　　　　　　　　　I'd love to, but ...「そうしたいのですが…」

●依頼する「〜してくれませんか」

Would you mind changing seats with me?——Not at all.
　　　　　　　　　　　　　（私と席を替わっていただけませんか。——構いませんよ。）
▷他の依頼の表現　Can［Could］/ Will you 〜?「〜してくれませんか［〜してくださいませんか］」
▷応答パターン　承諾　Sure.「もちろん」　My pleasure.「喜んで」　Certainly.「もちろん」
　　　　　　　　断り　I'm sorry, but I can't. / I'm afraid I can't.「残念ですが、できません」

●許可を求める「〜してもいいですか」

Can I take this seat?——Yes, please.（この席に座ってもいいですか。——ええ、どうぞ。）
▷他の許可の表現　May / Can I 〜?「〜してもよろしいですか」
▷応答パターン　承諾　Go ahead.「どうぞ」
　　　　　　　　断り　No, please don't.「いいえ、そうしないでください」
　　　　　　　　　　　I'm sorry, but you can't.「すみませんが、できません」

Try 1　次のタスクに取り組みましょう。

1　音声を聞き、質問文に対する最も適切な応答文を (A)〜(C) から選びましょう。　🎧32

　Ⓐ　Ⓑ　Ⓒ

2　もう一度音声を聞き、＿＿部分を埋めましょう。そして、1の答えを確認しましょう。　🎧32

　It's raining again. ＿＿＿＿ ＿＿＿＿ we ＿＿＿＿ a taxi?

　(A) I don't have a ＿＿＿＿ ＿＿＿＿.

　(B) ＿＿＿＿ ＿＿＿＿, but I don't know.

　(C) ＿＿＿＿ good.

Try 2

音声を聞き、____部分を埋めましょう。 🎧 33

1. _____ _____ _____ an _____ _____?
   —— I prefer a _____ _____.

2. _____ _____ check our _____ _____?
   —— _____ _____.

3. _____ _____ _____ the _____? It's fast.
   —— OK.

4. _____ _____ _____ our trip?
   —— _____ _____, but _____ _____
   any other _____ _____.

Try 3

音声を聞いて、質問文に対する最も適切な応答文を (A) 〜 (C) から選びましょう。 🎧 34-36

1. Ⓐ Ⓑ Ⓒ   2. Ⓐ Ⓑ Ⓒ   3. Ⓐ Ⓑ Ⓒ

Active Reading 🎧 37

目標：____秒　1回目：____秒　2回目：____秒

What is PRT?

Personal Rapid Transit (PRT) has been called the future of public transportation due to its eco-friendliness and speed. Most PRT systems have four to six passengers in each pod that are self-controlled to their destinations. Recent PRT systems have improved since the first one built in Morgantown, West Virginia, USA. The most recent system, MISTER, was built in Poland. The MISTER pods would be suspended in mid-air and powered electrically, and could carry 5,000 to 10,000 passengers for an hour in each direction at 50 kilometers per hour. Although PRT is good, there are a lot of political and technological problems. Anyway, it would be a nice idea that people in the future would be able to live in cities without cars.

語注　public transportation 公共交通機関　pod 車両　improve 改善する　suspend 浮かせる　electrically 電気によって

◆ 上の文章に合うように以下の空所を埋めましょう。

一般的な PRT は 1 つの車両に (¹　　　) 〜 (²　　　) 人の乗客を乗せて目的地まで自動運転で行く。ポーランドで開発された (³　　　) という PRT は 1 時間に (⁴　　　) 〜 (⁵　　　) 人の乗客を送迎でき、そのスピードは時速 (⁶　　　) キロである。

Reading Section

🔑 Key Point [Part 5 & 6] 前置詞

前置詞は、名詞（句）の前に置かれる品詞です。「場所」と「時間」を表す前置詞は頻出です。

場所を表す前置詞	at, in, to, by, from, on, over, out, above, under, below など
時間を表す前置詞	at, on, in, by, before, from, since, for, to, till, until, after など
その他よく出る前置詞	of, during, against, despite, within, without, about, with など

前置詞の後ろには名詞、名詞句※、動名詞が来ます。

 前置詞＋名詞 at home（自宅で）
 前置詞＋名詞句 by the end of the year（今年の末までに）
 前置詞＋動名詞 without saying goodbye（さよならを言わずに）

※「名詞句」とは、名詞と同じ働きをする2つ以上の語のまとまりのことです。

動詞や形容詞の中には、特定の前置詞とセットになるものがあります。

動詞	consist of ～	～を構成する
	count on ～	～を当てにする
	listen to ～	～を聞く
	look for ～	～を探す
	participate in ～	～に参加する
形容詞	be absent from ～	～を不在にしている
	be afraid of ～	～を恐れている
	be aware of ～	～を意識している
	be bound for ～	～行きである
	be similar to ～	～に似ている

📖 Try 1   次の英文の空所に入る最も適切な語句を選びましょう。

I plan to go by plane ------- Paris to London.
(A) of
(B) from
(C) before
(D) below

HINT 💡   場所を表す前置詞を考えましょう。
    （訳）私はパリからロンドンまで飛行機で移動しようと計画している。

Think / Write / Share

ペアまたはグループで協力してやりましょう。

A メンバーに昨日寝た時刻と今朝起きた時刻を尋ねて、その回答を書きましょう。時刻は前置詞 at を使います。

A: What time did you go to bed yesterday?
B: (例) *I went to bed at 11 p.m.* | _____
A: What time did you get up?
B: (例) *I got up at 8:30 a.m.* | _____

B メンバーに学校の行事の日程を尋ねて、その回答を書きましょう。日程や曜日には前置詞 on を使います。(**on** the 5th / **on** Monday)

A: What is the date of the school festival?
B: (例) *It is on November 5. / It is from November 5 to November 9.*

_____

C メンバーに今後の予定を尋ねて、その回答を書きましょう。月やそれより長い時間（季節、年）には前置詞 in を使います。(**in** November / **in** winter / **in** 2015)

A: What are you going to do in September?
B: (例) *I'm going to start a part-time job in September.*

_____

D メンバーに生まれた場所と育った場所を尋ねて、その回答を書きましょう。

A: Where were you born and raised?
B: (例) *I was born in Nakano, Tokyo and raised in Kashii, Fukuoka.*

_____

E メンバーに現住所と通学手段を尋ねて、その回答を書きましょう。(by train / on foot)

A: Where do you live now?
B: (例) *I live in Nagoya, Aichi.* | _____
A: How do you get to school?
B: (例) *I come here by bus.* | _____

Try 2 英文の空所に入る最も適切な語句を選びましょう。

1. Steven is listening ------- the departure time carefully.
   (A) by
   (B) at
   (C) to

2. The parking lot is away ------- the station.
   (A) from
   (B) in
   (C) with

3. I have to go ------- the stairs to change trains.
   (A) over
   (B) up
   (C) in

4. I'll see you ------- 9 a.m. and show you the way to the JR ticket counter.
   (A) down
   (B) at
   (C) by

5. Passengers are requested to fasten their seat belts ------- the flight.
   (A) from
   (B) during
   (C) on

6. This express train is bound ------- Oxford.
   (A) from
   (B) of
   (C) for

Try 3 英文の空所に入る最も適切な語句を選びましょう。

1. Be aware ------- pickpockets in the crowded subway.
   (A) by
   (B) of
   (C) at
   (D) in

2. We have a plan to participate ------- a jazz concert during the cruise.
   (A) by
   (B) in
   (C) of
   (D) with

3. I went to the lost and found ------- the station to look for my commuter pass.
   (A) with
   (B) on
   (C) at
   (D) for

4. Tim always counts ------- others, so he can't even say his destination.
   (A) of
   (B) to
   (C) in
   (D) on

Unit 6　Shopping

接続詞

Vocabulary

1 1〜20の語句を聞き取り、下の枠内から選んでA欄に書きましょう。

bargain	cash	credit card	cool	discount
expensive	fitting room	look for	on sale	pay
price	purchase	reasonable	receipt	register
return	stock	tax	try on	wrap

🎧 38　　A　　　　　B　　　　　🎧 39　　A　　　　　B

1. _____ _____　11. _____ _____
2. _____ _____　12. _____ _____
3. _____ _____　13. _____ _____
4. _____ _____　14. _____ _____
5. _____ _____　15. _____ _____
6. _____ _____　16. _____ _____
7. _____ _____　17. _____ _____
8. _____ _____　18. _____ _____
9. _____ _____　19. _____ _____
10. _____ _____　20. _____ _____

2 もう一度音声を聞き、1〜20の語句の意味を下の枠内から選んでB欄に書きましょう。

お買い得品	価格	かっこいい	クレジットカード	現金
高価な	購入する	在庫	試着室	支払う
税金	特価で	手頃な	返品する	包装する
領収書	レジ	割引をする	〜を探す	〜を試着する

Listening Section

🔑 Key Point　[Part 3] 設問の主語を押さえよう！

男性と女性の会話に基づいて答える Part 3 では、設問の主語が the man か the woman のどちらかになっている場合が多くあります。設問に目を通すときには、主語に注目し、男性と女性のどちらのことを問われているかを確認した上で、会話を聞きましょう。

W: Welcome to Hour Records. How can I help you?　　1. Where does the woman work?
　　　　　　　　　　　　　　　　　　　　　　　　　　（どこで、女性、働く）
M: I'm looking for a CD called *Love Songs*.
　　　　　　　　　　　　　　　　　　　　　　　2. What is the man looking for?
W: I can check for you. Do you know when it was　　　（何を、男性、探している）
　 released?
　　　　　　　　　　　　　　　　　　　　　　　3. What did the woman ask for?
M: In 2006 or 2007, maybe.　　　　　　　　　　　　　（何を、女性、求めている）

🔈 Try 1　次のタスクに取り組みましょう。

1 以下の設問の主語を◯で囲みましょう。

1. Why does the woman like the shirt?
2. What will the man probably do next?

2 2人の会話を聞き、**1** の設問の答えとして最も適切なものを選びましょう。　🎧 40

1. (A) She likes white.　　　　　　　　　2. (A) He will go and check the stock.
   (B) The design is not good.　　　　　　　 (B) He will check the price.
   (C) It is not expensive.　　　　　　　　　(C) He will try the shirt on.

3 もう一度会話を聞き、＿＿部分を埋めましょう。そして、**1** の答えを確認しましょう。　🎧 40

W: I ＿＿＿＿＿ this green ＿＿＿＿＿. The ＿＿＿＿＿ is so cool and the price

　 is ＿＿＿＿＿. Do you have it in ＿＿＿＿＿ ＿＿＿＿＿ ＿＿＿＿＿?

M: Let's see ... um ... we probably have the ＿＿＿＿＿ in brown and blue.

W: I'd ＿＿＿＿＿ the ＿＿＿＿＿ one.

M: Let me ＿＿＿＿＿ to see if we have any more ＿＿＿＿＿ ＿＿＿＿＿. I'll be back

　 soon.

Try 2　音声を聞き、＿＿部分を埋めましょう。　🎧 41

1. _____ _____ _____ _____ to _____? Credit card or _____?
2. I'd like to _____ _____ _____. _____ _____ the _____.
3. _____ is the _____ _____ _____ _____ this _____?
4. Many people are _____ _____ _____ _____ _____ _____ _____.

Try 3　2人の会話を聞き、設問の答えとして最も適切なものを選びましょう。　🎧 42

1. Where is this conversation most likely taking place?
   (A) In a bookstore
   (B) At a shop
   (C) At a café
   (D) On a bus

   Ⓐ Ⓑ Ⓒ Ⓓ

2. What does the woman mean when she says, "It's a deal"?
   (A) She likes the color.
   (B) She is thinking about buying it.
   (C) It was discounted.
   (D) It was popular.

   Ⓐ Ⓑ Ⓒ Ⓓ

3. What will the man probably do next?
   (A) Wrap the bag for the woman
   (B) Place the bag in the store window
   (C) Return the bag
   (D) Check the stock

   Ⓐ Ⓑ Ⓒ Ⓓ

Active Reading　🎧 43

目標：＿＿秒　1回目：＿＿秒　2回目：＿＿秒

Investment Shopping

Nicola Fumo recommends that some people learn "investment shopping," the practice of spending more money on quality than on quantity. If we use an item often, she suggests we focus more on quantity; if we use something only once in a while, she suggests emphasizing quality. She explains her point by comparing the price of a quality item that costs a lot to that of items that are a lot cheaper. For the price of a pair of designer shoes, one could buy six pairs of fast fashion shoes. Which would you prefer?

語注　recommend 勧める　practice 実践　emphasize 強調する　compare 比較する

◆ 上の文章に関する質問に答えましょう。

1. どのような場合に、量を重視すべきですか。　_____

2. ブランドものの靴1足で、ファストファッションの靴は何足買えると書いてありますか。_____足

Reading Section

🔑 Key Point ［Part 5 & 6］接続詞

接続詞は語と語、句と句、節と節をつなぎます。

［等位接続詞］　対等につなぎます。FANBOYS：F (for), A (and), N (nor), B (but), O (or), Y (yet), S (so) など。

　　　　　　　a shirt **and** a tie（シャツとネクタイ）
　　　　　　　pay in cash **or** by credit card（現金またはカードで支払う）
　　　　　　　I went shopping **but** I didn't buy anything.（買い物に行ったが、何も買わなかった。）

［従位接続詞］　主節に従属節をつなぎます。when「〜するとき」、if「もし〜すれば」、as「〜のときに」、because「なぜなら」、though「だけれども」、while「〜する間は」など。

　　　　　　　I bought a bottle of wine **because** it's pay day today.
　　　　　　　（今日は給料日なのでワインを1本買った。）

［名詞節をつくる接続詞］　**that、whether、if、while** などは、後ろに＜主語＋動詞＞を含む節を続けて「〜ということ」「〜かどうか」などの意味を表す名詞節をつくります。

　　　　　　　Emily cannot decide **whether** she should buy a gift for him.
　　　　　　　（エミリーは彼にプレゼントを買うべきか決められない。）

［節と句の違い］　節は＜主語＋動詞＞を含み、句は含みません。

接続詞と接続詞を含む前置詞句の用法の違い：TOEICの頻出ポイントの一つです。

接続詞＋節（＜主語＋動詞＞を含む）
<u>Because</u> it rained heavily, I gave up shopping.（雨がひどく降ったので、買い物をあきらめた。）

前置詞(句)＋名詞(句)
<u>Because of</u> the heavy rain, I gave up shopping.（ひどい雨のせいで、買い物をあきらめた。）

接続詞を含む慣用表現

both A and B	AとBの両方	so 〜 that ...	あまりに〜なので…
not A but B	AではなくB	not only A but also B	AだけでなくBも
either A or B	AかBのどちらか	neither A nor B	AもBも〜でない
命令文, and 〜	…しなさい、そうすれば〜	命令文, or 〜	…しなさい、さもないと〜

📖 Try 1　次の英文の空所に入る最も適切な語句を選びましょう。

------- I was looking around the shops, I found a very beautiful ring.

(A) And　　(B) During　　(C) Though　　(D) While

HINT 💡　コンマの前後の文の意味と、そのつながりについて考えましょう。
　　　　　（訳）お店を見て回っていたとき、とてもきれいな指輪を見つけた。

Think / Write / Share

ペアまたはグループで協力してやりましょう。

A <接続詞＋もう一文>で、文をつないでいきましょう。一番長い文をつくったグループの勝ちです。

（例）I bought an apple → and I ate it → but I'm still hungry

_____

_____

B 以下の語句を接続詞と前置詞（句）に分けましょう。

| in | by | if | when | during | because | because of | due to |
| owing to | instead of | despite | in spite of | although | while |

接続詞：_____

前置詞（句）：_____

C メンバーの持ち物を買った場所を尋ねて、その回答を書きましょう。それについてのコメントも付け加えましょう。

（例） A: Where did you buy your jacket?（質問）

B: I bought it at the KK department store because my mother recommended it.（回答）

A: It's cute and it suits you!（コメント）

質問：_____

回答：_____

コメント：_____

Try 2　英文の空所に入る最も適切な語句を選びましょう。

1. Hurry up, ------- you'll miss getting a bargain.
   (A) or
   (B) and
   (C) but

   Ⓐ Ⓑ Ⓒ

2. I bought a fan for my mother ------- Mother's Day.
   (A) because
   (B) because of
   (C) while

   Ⓐ Ⓑ Ⓒ

3. I'll buy this scarf ------- it's on sale.
   (A) when
   (B) but
   (C) for

4. I'll pay for it in cash ------- I forgot my credit card.
   (A) but
   (B) because
   (C) despite

5. Both red and pink are so pretty ------- I can't choose just one.
   (A) when
   (B) that
   (C) because

6. You can either pay now ------- later.
   (A) and
   (B) nor
   (C) or

Try 3

文章の4つの空所に入る最も適切な語句または文をそれぞれ選びましょう。

Dear Mrs. Lang:

Thank you for purchasing of a watch on July 18 and for signing up for a credit card with CGL Department Store. However, ---**1**.--- we checked your form, we found that your driver's license had expired, so we are unable to accept this form. We accept not only driver's licenses ---**2**.--- also other documents that prove identity, so could you please send us a copy of one of them?

---**3**.--- you have any questions about this, please contact our customer service. ---**4**.---

Sincerely,

Adam Willis
Customer Service, CGL Department Store

1. (A) if
   (B) yet
   (C) when
   (D) and

2. (A) but
   (B) and
   (C) so
   (D) as

3. (A) Because
   (B) If
   (C) But
   (D) Or

4. (A) We hope that you continue shopping at our store.
   (B) Our maintenance crew is already working.
   (C) You wanted us to explain about the problem.
   (D) I belong to the sales department.

Unit 7 Restaurant

不定詞 1

Vocabulary

1 1〜20の語句を聞き取り、下の枠内から選んでA欄に書きましょう。

be full of	beverage	crowded	dish	eat out
empty	fast-food restaurant	fork	in line	knife
meal	offer	order	pile up	raw fish
satisfy	scatter	service charge	side by side	tip

🎧 44   A   B   🎧 45   A   B

1. _____ _____   11. _____ _____
2. _____ _____   12. _____ _____
3. _____ _____   13. _____ _____
4. _____ _____   14. _____ _____
5. _____ _____   15. _____ _____
6. _____ _____   16. _____ _____
7. _____ _____   17. _____ _____
8. _____ _____   18. _____ _____
9. _____ _____   19. _____ _____
10. _____ _____   20. _____ _____

2 もう一度音声を聞き、1〜20の語句の意味を下の枠内から選んでB欄に書きましょう。

一列で	飲料	外食する	空の	混んだ
サービス料	食事	チップ	注文する	積み上げる
提供する	〜でいっぱいである	ナイフ	生魚	ファーストフード店
フォーク	まき散らす	満足させる	横に並んで	料理

Listening Section

Key Point [Part 1] 人や物の様子・状態を表す定型表現を押さえよう！

受動態 (be + 過去分詞) を用いた定型表現

be covered with ～「～で覆われている」	be full of ～ / be filled with ～「～でいっぱいである」
be piled up on ～「～に積み上げられている」	be scattered on ～「～に散らばっている」
be set on ～「～に置かれている」	be hung on ～「～に掛けられている」

その他のよく使われる表現

in line「一列で[に]」	on the line「電話中で」
under construction「建設中で」	lean against ～「～に寄りかかる」
face each other「向かい合う」	side by side「横に並んで、隣同士で」

Try 1   次のタスクに取り組みましょう。

1 音声を聞いて、右の写真の様子を最もよく表している
　 ものを (A) 〜 (C) より1つ選びましょう。　🎧 46

　　　　　　　　　　Ⓐ　Ⓑ　Ⓒ

2 もう一度音声を聞き、＿＿部分を埋めましょう。そして、1 の答えを確認しましょう。　🎧 46

(A) The _____ are _____ _____ _____ to get their _____.

(B) The _____ _____ and the _____ are _____ _____ _____.

(C) Many _____ are _____ _____ on the tray.

Try 2   音声を聞き、＿＿部分を埋めましょう。　🎧 47

1. _____ and _____ are _____ _____ the table.

2. The _____ _____ is _____ _____ _____.

3. Some _____ _____ _____ _____ _____ _____ the _____.

4. _____ kinds of _____ _____ _____ the _____.

58 | Unit 7 Restaurant   不定詞 1

Try 3

音声を聞いて、それぞれの写真の様子を最もよく表している英文を選びましょう。

48-50

1.
Ⓐ Ⓑ Ⓒ Ⓓ

2. 3.
Ⓐ Ⓑ Ⓒ Ⓓ Ⓐ Ⓑ Ⓒ Ⓓ

Active Reading　🎧 51

目標：＿＿秒　1回目：＿＿秒　2回目：＿＿秒

The Trouble with Tipping

Tipping has been a confusing part of travel for many tourists, especially in the US where it is most common. There is no one rule for how much to tip, or who to tip. Many people think that tipping should be replaced by a service charge because it is inconvenient for patrons and it has become more of a social obligation than a reward for good service. However, since a service charge might remove the incentive to provide good service, it could still take time before tipping is replaced.

語注　confusing 紛らわしい　common 一般的な　replace 取って代わる　patron 常連　obligation 義務　incentive やる気

◆ 以下が上の文章に合っていればT、間違っていればFを [　] に書きましょう。Fの場合は訂正しましょう。

1. [　] チップの金額やチップを渡す相手についてのルールがある。
2. [　] 多くの人が、チップはサービス料に代わるべきだと思っている。

Reading Section

Key Point ［Part 5 & 6］不定詞 1：to 不定詞の用法

<to + 動詞の原形>は不定詞（to 不定詞）と呼ばれ、次の 3 つの用法があります。

名詞的用法	～すること	It is fun **to eat** out.（外食は楽しい。）
形容詞的用法	～するための	I ordered something **to drink**.（飲み物を注文した。）
副詞的用法	～するために	I visited a restaurant **to see** her.（彼女に会うためにレストランを訪れた。）

不定詞を使った重要構文

It is ... for A to *do*	「～することは A にとって…である」

It is very **exciting for Mike to eat** out with her.
（彼女と外食することはマイクにとって、とても胸が踊ることだ。）

too ... to *do*	「あまりに…なので～しない（できない）」

Mike was **too nervous to talk** much with her at the restaurant.
（マイクはとても緊張したので、レストランで彼女とあまり話すことができなかった。）

in order to *do* ／ so as to *do*	「～するために」

Mike ordered expensive dishes **so as to look** cool.
（マイクはかっこつけるために、高い料理を注文した。）

to tell the truth	「実を言うと」
... enough to *do*	「～するのに十分な…」

To tell the truth, Mike wasn't rich **enough to pay** for them.
（実を言うと、マイクはそれらを支払うのに十分なほど金持ちではなかった。）

<疑問詞＋to 不定詞>

how to *do*	～のやり方	when to *do*	いつ～する(べき)か
what to *do*	何を～する(べき)か	which to *do*	どちらを～する(べき)か
where to *do*	どこで～する(べき)か		

Try 1　次の英文の空所に入る最も適切な語句を選びましょう。

I'll be back in a few minutes ------- take your order.

(A) how
(B) after
(C) it
(D) to

HINT　空所の直後が動詞の原形になっています。
（訳）数分後、ご注文を伺いに戻ってまいります。

Think / Write / Share

ペアまたはグループで協力してやりましょう。

A この先あなたがしたいことをwantを用いて書いてみましょう。

(例) I want to go around the world.

___

B A で考えた自分の目標を叶えるために必要なステップを考えて書きましょう。

ステップ1：(例) I study English in order to go around the world.

___

ステップ2：(例) I listen to the lecture carefully so as to study English in order to go around the world.

> クラスで一番長い文を書いた人は誰でしょう？

___
___
___

Try 2
英文の空所に入る最も適切な語句を選びましょう。

1. Paul opened the restaurant ------- make his dream come true.
   - (A) be
   - (B) do
   - (C) to

   Ⓐ Ⓑ Ⓒ

2. It's good for us to ------- organic food.
   - (A) eat
   - (B) ate
   - (C) eating

   Ⓐ Ⓑ Ⓒ

3. This steak is ------- tough for me to eat.
   - (A) to
   - (B) too
   - (C) very

   Ⓐ Ⓑ Ⓒ

4. Lunchtime is so busy that he needs someone ------- him.
   - (A) to help
   - (B) help
   - (C) to have helped

   Ⓐ Ⓑ Ⓒ

5. Linda had no idea about ------- to cook for him.
   - (A) so
   - (B) why
   - (C) what

   Ⓐ Ⓑ Ⓒ

6. I'd like to have something -------.
   - (A) drink
   - (B) drinking
   - (C) to drink

   Ⓐ Ⓑ Ⓒ

Try 3 英文の空所に入る最も適切な語句を選びましょう。

1. I'm happy to ------- that you like this meal.
   (A) heard
   (B) hearing
   (C) hear
   (D) hears

2. I don't know ------- to order at the café.
   (A) have
   (B) take
   (C) how
   (D) had

3. He went to France in ------- to work in a French restaurant.
   (A) order
   (B) for
   (C) so
   (D) as

4. The food at the cafeteria was good ------- satisfy us.
   (A) at
   (B) so to
   (C) enough to
   (D) much to

5. To tell the -------, I can't eat raw fish.
   (A) true
   (B) truth
   (C) story
   (D) stories

6. The restaurant was ------- crowded to have a relaxing dinner.
   (A) to
   (B) too
   (C) much
   (D) many

7. The chef is working very hard so ------- to offer delicious food.
   (A) as
   (B) too
   (C) where
   (D) when

8. We are not allowed ------- during dinner.
   (A) smoking
   (B) to smoke
   (C) so as to smoke
   (D) how to smoke

Unit 8 Entertainment

不定詞2

Vocabulary

1 1〜20の語句を聞き取り、下の枠内から選んでA欄に書きましょう。

actor	amusement park	audience	available	be sold out
championship game	concert	event	excited	famous
last	movie theater	on TV	performance	popular
spectator	stadium	ticket	video game	wonderful

🎧 52   A   B   🎧 53   A   B

1. _____ _____   11. _____ _____
2. _____ _____   12. _____ _____
3. _____ _____   13. _____ _____
4. _____ _____   14. _____ _____
5. _____ _____   15. _____ _____
6. _____ _____   16. _____ _____
7. _____ _____   17. _____ _____
8. _____ _____   18. _____ _____
9. _____ _____   19. _____ _____
10. _____ _____   20. _____ _____

2 もう一度音声を聞き、1〜20の語句の意味を下の枠内から選んでB欄に書きましょう。

売り切れる	映画館	演技	決勝戦	(劇場などの)観客
興奮している	コンサート	スタジアム	素晴らしい	(スポーツなどの)観客
チケット	続く	テレビゲーム	テレビで	入手できる
人気がある	催し物	役者	遊園地	有名な

Listening Section

Key Point　[Part 2]　付加疑問文・否定疑問文への答え方に慣れよう！

付加疑問文と否定疑問文に対する応答文では、Noで「はい」、Yesで「いいえ」という意味になるときがあります。

普通の疑問文	Does he play video games every day? （彼は毎日テレビゲームをしますか。）	Yes, he does. （はい、します。）	No, he doesn't. （いいえ、しません。）
付加疑問文	You saw the movie, **didn't you**? （その映画を観ましたよね？）	Yes, I did. （はい、観ました。）	No, I didn't. （いいえ、観ませんでした。）
	The ticket *isn't* available, **is it**? （チケットは入手できませんよね？）	Yes, it is. （いいえ、入手できます。）	No, it isn't. （はい、入手できません。）
否定疑問文	**Didn't** you go to the stadium? （スタジアムに行かなかったんですか。）	Yes, I did. （いいえ、行きました。）	No, I didn't. （はい、行きませんでした。）

Try 1　次のタスクに取り組みましょう。

1　音声を聞いて、質問文に対する最も適切な応答文を (A) 〜 (C) から選びましょう。　🎧 54

　Ⓐ　Ⓑ　Ⓒ

2　もう一度音声を聞き、＿＿部分を埋めましょう。そして、1の答えを確認しましょう。　🎧 54

＿＿＿＿＿＿ you go to the ＿＿＿＿＿＿ ＿＿＿＿＿＿ yesterday?

(A) ＿＿＿＿＿＿, I did. I was so ＿＿＿＿＿＿ yesterday with my ＿＿＿＿＿＿.

(B) ＿＿＿＿＿＿, I did. I ＿＿＿＿＿＿ ＿＿＿＿＿＿ with my friend.

(C) ＿＿＿＿＿＿, I didn't. I saw a famous musician at the ＿＿＿＿＿＿ ＿＿＿＿＿＿.

Try 2　音声を聞き、＿＿部分を埋めましょう。　🎧 55

1. ＿＿＿＿＿＿ you ＿＿＿＿＿＿ the ＿＿＿＿＿＿?

　—— ＿＿＿＿＿＿, I do. I love his songs.

2. ＿＿＿＿＿＿ ＿＿＿＿＿＿ ＿＿＿＿＿＿ the musical?

　—— I ＿＿＿＿＿＿ ＿＿＿＿＿＿ ＿＿＿＿＿＿ ＿＿＿＿＿＿.

3. The ＿＿＿＿＿＿ ＿＿＿＿＿＿ ＿＿＿＿＿＿ ＿＿＿＿＿＿ ＿＿＿＿＿＿ ＿＿＿＿＿＿, didn't it?

　—— ＿＿＿＿＿＿, I was ＿＿＿＿＿＿.

4. Didn't the _____ _____ _____ about the actor's _____?

—— It wasn't that great.

5. The _____ is supposed to be _____ _____ _____ _____, _____ _____?

—— Yes, it starts at 6 p.m.

Try 3 音声を聞いて、質問文に対する最も適切な応答文を (A) 〜 (C) から選びましょう。 56-58

1. Ⓐ Ⓑ Ⓒ   2. Ⓐ Ⓑ Ⓒ   3. Ⓐ Ⓑ Ⓒ

Active Reading 59

目標：____ 秒　1回目：____ 秒　2回目：____ 秒

The Weekly Package

Many people around the world can easily access the Internet not just from their homes but also from their pockets. In Cuba, Internet access is expensive and slow, many people do not have a mobile phone, and cable and satellite TV are not allowed in homes. However, they can get the latest media, apps and games at home thanks to the "Weekly Package." People who have access to the Internet download one terabyte's worth of the latest multimedia and divide them into external hard drives and memory sticks to be sold to those who want them, at about $6 for everything. Also, it becomes half price after two days.

語注　expensive 高価な　latest 最新の　thanks to 〜 〜のおかげで　divide 分ける　external 外付けの

◆ 上の文章に関する質問に日本語で答えましょう。

1. インターネット環境の整備が遅れているキューバで、人々が最新のテレビ番組やゲームを楽しめるのは、何というシステムがあるからでしょうか。

2. 1. で答えたシステムの使用料はいくらですか。

Reading Section

🔑 Key Point ［Part 5 & 6］ 不定詞２：不定詞をとる動詞

不定詞だけをとる動詞

agree to *do*	「～することに同意する」	manage to *do*	「なんとか～する」
decide to *do*	「～することに決める」	offer to *do*	「～することを申し出る」
expect to *do*	「～することを期待する」	plan to *do*	「～する予定である」
fail to *do*	「～し損なう」	pretend to *do*	「～するふりをする」
hope to *do*	「～することを望む」	refuse to *do*	「～することを断る」
learn to *do*	「～することを学ぶ」	wish to *do*	「～したいと願う」

不定詞と動名詞の両方をとって意味が変わる動詞

stop to *do*「止まって～する」	stop *doing*「～するのをやめる」
He stopped to sing.（彼は立ち止まって歌った。）	He stopped singing.（彼は歌うのをやめた。）
forget to *do*「～し忘れる」	forget *doing*「～したことを忘れる」
She'll never forget to see the actor. （彼女はその役者に会うことを決して忘れないだろう。）	She'll never forget seeing the actor. （彼女はその役者に会ったことを決して忘れないだろう。）
remember to *do*「忘れずに～する」	remember *doing*「～したことを覚えている」
Please remember to buy the CD. （忘れずに CD を買ってきてください。）	I remember buying the CD. （私は CD を買ったことを覚えている。）

📖 **Try 1**　次の英文の空所に入る最も適切な語句を選びましょう。

I'm planning ------- to the amusement park with her.

(A) going
(B) to go
(C) goes
(D) gone

HINT　plan は後ろに何をとる動詞でしょうか。
（訳）私は彼女と遊園地に行くことを計画している。

ペアまたはグループで協力してやりましょう。

A 与えられた書き出しのあとに動詞の原形を続けて文をつくりましょう。できた文をシェアしましょう。

（例）I decided to talk to him.（私は彼に話しかけることに決めた。）

1. I decided to _____

2. I expect to _____

3. I hope to _____

4. I learned to _____

5. I manage to _____

6. I plan to _____

B 次の英文を意味の違いに気をつけて訳しましょう。

1. My sister remembers to go to the movie theater.
   訳：(   )

2. My sister remembers going to the movie theater.
   訳：(   )

C 不定詞と動名詞の訳の違いはどういったイメージの違いから来るのか話し合ってみましょう。

(   )

Unit 8 Entertainment 不定詞2

Try 2　英文の空所に入る最も適切な語句を選びましょう。

1. Bill managed ------- a ticket for the championship game.
   (A) got
   (B) getting
   (C) to get
   Ⓐ Ⓑ Ⓒ

2. I wish ------- a pop star.
   (A) am
   (B) to be
   (C) to
   Ⓐ Ⓑ Ⓒ

3. He ------- to make her a star because of her performance.
   (A) decided
   (B) denied
   (C) advised
   Ⓐ Ⓑ Ⓒ

4. A huge crowd of spectators ------- to see a home run to end the game.
   (A) enjoyed
   (B) expected
   (C) gave up
   Ⓐ Ⓑ Ⓒ

Try 3　文章の4つの空所に入る最も適切な語句または文をそれぞれ選びましょう。

From:　　Nicole Lang
To:　　　Tom Costello
Date:　　November 5
Subject:　The party

Hi Tom,

Thank you so much ---**1**.--- me to the party this coming Friday. Everyone is excited about the event and I hope that everyone can attend.

I'm happy that you have ---**2**.--- to go with me. I expect ---**3**.--- have a wonderful time there with you. ---**4**.---

Nicole

1. (A) for inviting
   (B) to invite
   (C) invite
   (D) inviting
   Ⓐ Ⓑ Ⓒ Ⓓ

2. (A) decided
   (B) enjoyed
   (C) considered
   (D) suggested
   Ⓐ Ⓑ Ⓒ Ⓓ

3. (A) for
   (B) to
   (C) at
   (D) in
   Ⓐ Ⓑ Ⓒ Ⓓ

4. (A) It will give your guests free drinks.
   (B) I'm looking forward to it!
   (C) Let me know by Friday.
   (D) You are interested in the party.
   Ⓐ Ⓑ Ⓒ Ⓓ

Unit 9 Trouble
動名詞

Vocabulary

1 1〜20の語句を聞き取り、下の枠内から選んでA欄に書きましょう。

advise	apologize	avoid	belongings	careful
deny	embassy	fail	forget	leave
lost	mind	miss	passport	pickpocket
postpone	prevent	refund	refuse	trouble

🎧 60　　A　　　　B

1. _____　_____
2. _____　_____
3. _____　_____
4. _____　_____
5. _____　_____
6. _____　_____
7. _____　_____
8. _____　_____
9. _____　_____
10. _____　_____

🎧 61　　A　　　　B

11. _____　_____
12. _____　_____
13. _____　_____
14. _____　_____
15. _____　_____
16. _____　_____
17. _____　_____
18. _____　_____
19. _____　_____
20. _____　_____

2 もう一度音声を聞き、1〜20の語句の意味を下の枠内から選んでB欄に書きましょう。

謝る	延期する	置き忘れる	気にする	拒否する
避ける	妨げる	失敗する	助言する	所持品
すり	大使館	注意深い	トラブル	逃す
パスポート	払い戻し	否定する	道に迷った	忘れる

Listening Section

Key Point [Part 3] 会話の流れに沿って設問のヒントを探そう！

Part 3 の会話問題にはそれぞれ設問が 3 つありますが、1 つ目の設問は会話の冒頭、2 つ目は中間、3 つ目は終盤から正答を導くことができるようになっている場合が大半です。

W: Oh, the air conditioner in this room is broken. It doesn't work on such a cold day. ← 1. What is the trouble with the room?

M: Yes. I called the front desk twice to come and look at it, but nobody has come. ← 2. What has the man done twice?

W: I guess we should ask for another room.

M: Yes. But I'm afraid there is no vacancy. ← 3. What is the man worried about?

Try 1 次のタスクに取り組みましょう。 (p.34を見よう)

1 会話の音声が流れる前に、まず以下の設問の聞き取りポイントをまとめましょう。

1. Where is this conversation most likely taking place? （   ）

2. What is the woman's problem? （   ）

3. What does the man suggest she do? （   ）

2 会話を聞き、1 の設問の答えとして最も適切なものを選びましょう。　🎧 62

1. (A) At a gym
   (B) At a restaurant
   (C) At a museum

2. (A) She lost her belongings.
   (B) She is lost.
   (C) She has a stomachache.

3. (A) To look carefully
   (B) To get the bag back
   (C) To go to the police

3 もう一度音声を聞き、＿＿部分を埋めましょう。そして、2 の答えを確認しましょう。　🎧 62

W: ＿＿＿＿＿ ＿＿＿＿＿ ＿＿＿＿＿ my bag? I had ＿＿＿＿＿ at this restaurant earlier and I ＿＿＿＿＿ it here.

M: Which ＿＿＿＿＿ were you at?

W: That one over there. Oh, I ＿＿＿＿＿ ＿＿＿＿＿ my ＿＿＿＿＿ there. All my ＿＿＿＿＿ ― my passport, my wallet, and my cellphone ― were in the bag. What should I do?

M: I think that you should go to the ＿＿＿＿＿.

Try 2 音声を聞き、＿＿部分を埋めましょう。 🎧 63

1. Please _____ _____ of _____ _____.
2. I _____ _____ _____ _____ _____ _____.
3. _____ _____, but I think _____ _____.
4. If you _____ _____ _____, go to the _____ _____.

Try 3 3人の会話を聞き、設問の答えとして最も適切なものを選びましょう。 🎧 64

1. What happened to the man?
   (A) He was lost in the airport.
   (B) He missed the shuttle bus.
   (C) He couldn't find his luggage.
   (D) He left his luggage in the plane.
   Ⓐ Ⓑ Ⓒ Ⓓ

2. When will the man fly to Fukuoka?
   (A) Tomorrow
   (B) Tonight
   (C) In 45 minutes
   (D) In two hours
   Ⓐ Ⓑ Ⓒ Ⓓ

3. Why does the man say, "I can't believe this"?
   (A) He is pleasantly surprised.
   (B) He can finally get his suitcase back.
   (C) He feels frustrated.
   (D) He is very busy.
   Ⓐ Ⓑ Ⓒ Ⓓ

Active Reading 🎧 65

目標：＿＿秒　1回目：＿＿秒　2回目：＿＿秒

How to Avoid Travel Troubles

Here are some tips shared by Kevin Lee, a university student who went to Malaysia for an internship. Only pack what you need so you can travel a lot easier. Do not bring expensive items. Know where your belongings are at all times. Keep items where they are safe. Make friends with your roommates and keep in contact with them. These new friends could help make your future travels easier. Read about the culture of the country you are visiting and be respectful of the people there. Travel in groups so that you do not get lost. It makes your traveling safer and more fun.

語注　tip 助言　pack 詰める　respectful 敬意を表す

◆ 旅行での持ち物について、上の文章に書かれている助言をまとめましょう。

Reading Section

🔑 Key Point ［Part 5 & 6］動名詞

動名詞は動詞にingを付けた形で、「～すること」という意味で名詞の働きをする語のことです。

fix（修理する）→ fix**ing**（修理すること）

Fixing a problem quickly is important.（問題を迅速に解決することが大切だ。）

動名詞だけをとる動詞（句）

advise *doing*	「～することを助言する」	give up *doing*	「～するのをやめる / あきらめる」
avoid *doing*	「～するのを避ける」	mind *doing*	「～するのをいやがる / 気にする」
consider *doing*	「～することをよく考える」	miss *doing*	「～し損なう」
deny *doing*	「～することを否定する」	postpone / put off *doing*	「～することを延期する」
enjoy *doing*	「～するのを楽しむ」	practice *doing*	「～するのを練習する」
finish *doing*	「～するのを終える」	suggest *doing*	「～することを勧める」

動名詞を含む慣用表現

be worth *doing*	～する価値がある
cannot help *doing*	～せざるを得ない
feel like *doing*	～したい
prevent A from *doing*	Aが～することを妨げる
It is no use *doing*.	～しても無駄である。
Would you mind *doing*?	～していただけますか。

📖 Try 1　次の英文の空所に入る最も適切な語句を選びましょう。

She avoided ------- to the dangerous area.

(A) go
(B) to go
(C) going
(D) have gone

HINT 🔍　avoidは後ろに何をとる動詞でしょうか。
（訳）彼女は危険な場所へ行くことを避けた。

Think / Write / Share

ペアまたはグループで協力してやりましょう。

A 後ろに①不定詞だけをとる動詞(句)、②動名詞だけをとる動詞(句)、そして③不定詞・動名詞の両方をとって意味が変わる動詞(句)に分けましょう。

p.66を見よう

advise	agree	avoid	consider	decide	deny	enjoy
expect	fail	finish	forget	give up	hope	learn
manage	mind	miss	offer	plan	postpone	practice
pretend	refuse	remember	stop	suggest	wish	

① 不定詞だけをとる動詞(句)［12語］

_____

_____

② 動名詞だけをとる動詞(句)［12語］

_____

_____

③ 両方をとって意味が変わる動詞(句)［3語］

_____

B (　)内の動詞を適切な形に直しましょう。

1. I'm good at (ask) _____ people.

2. We look forward to (receive) _____ better service next time.

   HINT この to は前置詞で、不定詞の to ではありません。

3. Tim left home without (lock) _____ the door.

C B の 1 ～ 3 の文にある構文上の共通点を考えましょう。

(　　　　　　　　　　　　　　　　　　　　　　　　　　　　　　)

Try 2 英文の空所に入る最も適切な語句を選びましょう。

1. He postponed ------- for America because of the accident.
   (A) leave
   (B) to leave
   (C) leaving
   Ⓐ Ⓑ Ⓒ

2. Hugh ------- her to call the police.
   (A) advised
   (B) planned
   (C) agreed
   Ⓐ Ⓑ Ⓒ

3. You should avoid ------- cash during the trip.
   (A) carries
   (B) carrying
   (C) to carry
   Ⓐ Ⓑ Ⓒ

4. Bill decided to give up ------- for his health.
   (A) drink
   (B) drinks
   (C) drinking
   Ⓐ Ⓑ Ⓒ

5. He ------- taking the wallet from her bag.
   (A) denied
   (B) decided
   (C) desired
   Ⓐ Ⓑ Ⓒ

6. Nicole always puts off ------- important tasks.
   (A) to do
   (B) does
   (C) doing
   Ⓐ Ⓑ Ⓒ

Try 3 次の英文の空所に入る最も適切な語句を選びましょう。

1. She has forgotten ------- here.
   (A) to come
   (B) come
   (C) comes
   (D) coming
   Ⓐ Ⓑ Ⓒ Ⓓ

2. The fog prevented us ------- seeing very far.
   (A) and
   (B) from
   (C) in
   (D) with
   Ⓐ Ⓑ Ⓒ Ⓓ

3. She seriously ------- asking for a refund.
   (A) agreed
   (B) determined
   (C) considered
   (D) promised
   Ⓐ Ⓑ Ⓒ Ⓓ

4. I remember ------- a lot of trouble in that city.
   (A) have
   (B) has
   (C) to have
   (D) having
   Ⓐ Ⓑ Ⓒ Ⓓ

Unit 10　Office 1

分詞

Vocabulary

1. 1〜20の語句を聞き取り、下の枠内から選んでA欄に書きましょう。

annual report	branch	business trip	CEO	client
colleague	company	copier	document	employee
headquarters	hire	leave a message	manager	manual
office	president	refill	take a day off	uniform

🎧 66　　A　　　　　　B

1. _____ _____
2. _____ _____
3. _____ _____
4. _____ _____
5. _____ _____
6. _____ _____
7. _____ _____
8. _____ _____
9. _____ _____
10. _____ _____

🎧 67　　A　　　　　　B

11. _____ _____
12. _____ _____
13. _____ _____
14. _____ _____
15. _____ _____
16. _____ _____
17. _____ _____
18. _____ _____
19. _____ _____
20. _____ _____

2. もう一度音声を聞き、1〜20の語句の意味を下の枠内から選んでB欄に書きましょう。

一日休みをとる	会社	顧客	コピー機	最高経営責任者
支社	事務所	社長	従業員	出張
書類	制服	詰め替え品	伝言を残す	同僚
取扱い説明書	年次報告	部長	本部	雇う

Listening Section

Key Point ［Part 3］ 語句の言い換え（パラフレーズ）を見抜こう！

Part 4 にも有効！

設問や選択肢では、会話文の中で使われた語句と同じ意味・内容を表す別の語句が用いられることがあります。

同僚	colleague – coworker	社長	president – head
部長	head – manager	本社・本部	headquarters – main office
計画	plan – project	雇う	employ – hire
話し合う	discuss – talk about	増える	increase – rise
取りやめる	cancel – call off	故障して	out of order – broken
うれしい	happy – pleased	取扱い説明書	manual – instruction book

Try 1 次のタスクに取り組みましょう。

1 2人の会話を聞き、設問の答えとして最も適切なものを選びましょう。　🎧 68

1. What did Henry call off?
   (A) Going to the bookstore
   (B) A business trip
   (C) A meeting

2. What will they do on Monday?
   (A) They will discuss a new plan.
   (B) They will exchange books.
   (C) They will go lunch together.

2 もう一度音声を聞き、＿＿部分を埋めましょう。そして、**1**の答えを確認しましょう。　🎧 68

W: CGL Publications. How may I help you?

M: Hi, This is John Smith of Tatsuya Bookstore. I'd like to ＿＿＿＿＿＿ ＿＿＿＿＿＿ Henry, please.

W: Oh, John. Henry is out for a meeting and ＿＿＿＿＿＿ ＿＿＿＿＿＿ ＿＿＿＿＿＿ for you. He said that he ＿＿＿＿＿＿ his ＿＿＿＿＿＿ ＿＿＿＿＿＿, so he could ＿＿＿＿＿＿ you next ＿＿＿＿＿＿.

M: Great. We'll talk about a new project ＿＿＿＿＿＿.

Try 2 音声を聞き、____ 部分を埋めましょう。 🎧 69

1. Our _____ will _____ _____ _____ _____.

2. I was _____ to _____ that one of my _____ _____
   _____.

3. We will _____ _____ _____ _____ _____.

4. Our _____ is in Tokyo and _____ _____ _____ _____
   in Japan.

Try 3 2人の会話を聞き、設問の答えとして最も適切なものを選びましょう。 🎧 70

1. What is the problem?
   (A) The boss got angry.
   (B) There are no refills.
   (C) The copier ran out of ink.
   (D) The manual is difficult.
   Ⓐ Ⓑ Ⓒ Ⓓ

2. Where are they most likely talking now?
   (A) At their desks
   (B) At the office
   (C) At a station
   (D) In the elevator
   Ⓐ Ⓑ Ⓒ Ⓓ

3. Why did the woman say she could change the ink refill?
   (A) She looked at a sign.
   (B) The man told her how to do it.
   (C) She asked her boss to change it.
   (D) She found the manual.
   Ⓐ Ⓑ Ⓒ Ⓓ

Active Reading 🎧 71

目標：____ 秒　1回目：____ 秒　2回目：____ 秒

Office Telephone Etiquette

It is always good to be more polite than usual when answering or making office phone calls. Here are a few things you can try. When answering the phone, greet the caller and say the name of the company and of the department before saying your name. When making a call, say your name before your company's, then ask to speak to your contact person. Try to sit or stand up straight while speaking on the phone to speak clearly. Expect to be put on voice-mail when you call, and be ready to leave a message by writing down everything you want to say.

語注　etiquette エチケット　polite 丁寧な　contact person（連絡）担当者

◆ 会社の電話に出るとき、以下の項目をどの順番で言うべきですか。[ ] に番号を書きましょう。

自分の名前 [　]　　あいさつ [　]　　部署名 [　]　　会社名 [　]

Reading Section

Key Point ［Part 5 & 6］ 分詞

分詞は動詞の意味合いを持ちながら、名詞を修飾します（形容詞的な働きをする）。次の2種類があります。

現在分詞	動詞＋ing	a **talking** man （話している男性）
過去分詞	動詞＋ed（不規則動詞の過去分詞形）	a **repaired** copier （修理されたコピー機）

現在分詞と過去分詞は、次のように使い分けます。

　　　分詞の意味上の主語が「する」→　現在分詞：a man が talk する
　　　　　　　　　　　　　　「される」→　過去分詞：a copier が repair される

分詞が1語の場合は名詞の前から、分詞が語句を伴って2語以上の句になる場合は名詞の後ろから修飾します。

　　　a talking man（話している人）　　　a man talking with Bill（ビルと一緒に話している人）

注意 「〜させる」動詞の分詞

次の動詞は、現在分詞が物事について「〜させる」、過去分詞が人について「〜する」という意味になり、普通の動詞とは意味合いが逆になります。

amaze「びっくりさせる」	please「喜ばせる」
bore「退屈させる」	satisfy「満足させる」
disappoint「がっかりさせる」	surprise「驚かせる」
excite「興奮させる」	tire「疲れさせる」

　　I saw an **exciting** concert.　（私は興奮させるコンサートを見た。）
　　I saw an **excited** audience.　（私は興奮する聴衆を見た。）

Try 1　次の英文の空所に入る最も適切な語句を選びましょう。

The client ------- at the entrance is waiting to see the president.
(A) stand
(B) stood
(C) standing
(D) stands

HINT　空所に入る語はclientを修飾します。
　　　　　（訳）入口に立っている顧客は、社長に会うために待っている。

Think / Write / Share

ペアまたはグループで協力してやりましょう。

A 1〜6を訳しましょう。

1. a ringing telephone
   訳：(   )

2. a colored poster
   訳：(   )

3. an exciting championship game
   訳：(   )

4. an excited actor
   訳：(   )

5. an operator disappointed with her salary
   訳：(   )

6. a receptionist bored at her desk
   訳：(   )

B 1〜4の____部分に名詞を入れて、訳しましょう。

1. a sleeping _____
   訳：(   )

2. a canceled _____
   訳：(   )

3. a disappointing _____
   訳：(   )

4. a bored _____
   訳：(   )

Try 2　英文の空所に入る最も適切な語句を選びましょう。

1. That woman ------- a uniform is our employee.
   (A) wear
   (B) wearing
   (C) wore
   　　　　　　Ⓐ Ⓑ Ⓒ

2. She took a day off today because of an ------- accident.
   (A) expecting
   (B) expect
   (C) unexpected
   　　　　　　Ⓐ Ⓑ Ⓒ

3. The company started to use brochure ------- in China.
   (A) print
   (B) prints
   (C) printed
   　　　　　　Ⓐ Ⓑ Ⓒ

4. The ------- president proudly announced their annual report.
   (A) satisfied
   (B) satisfies
   (C) satisfying
   　　　　　　Ⓐ Ⓑ Ⓒ

5. There are many newly ------- employees in the main office.
   (A) hiring
   (B) hired
   (C) hire

6. My boss gave me the data ------- the results.
   (A) shows
   (B) shown
   (C) showing

Try 3
文章の4つの空所に入る最も適切な語または文をそれぞれ選びましょう。

From: ajackson@goodwill.com
To: jharrison@goodwill.com
Date: Thursday, October 1
Subject: Paternity leave and pay

Dear Ms. Harrison,

I'm applying to take time off work from November 10 to support my wife and care for our baby. I'd like to receive my paternity pay from this date. Please review the ---**1**.--- documents.

I'm now involved in a big project ---**2**.--- for this town, so I think one week of paternity leave is maximum for me.

I hope that I have a ---**3**.--- good relationship with my department. ---**4**.---

Kind regards,
Adam Jackson

1. (A) attach
   (B) attaching
   (C) attaches
   (D) attached

2. (A) work
   (B) works
   (C) working
   (D) worked

3. (A) continues
   (B) continued
   (C) continuing
   (D) to be continued

4. (A) I will be happy to assist you.
   (B) Thank you and I hope to hear from you soon.
   (C) I look forward to my vacation next week.
   (D) My family wants a new house.

Unit 11　Office 2

仮定法

Vocabulary

1　1〜20の語句を聞き取り、下の枠内から選んでA欄に書きましょう。

against	agenda	apply for	appointment	budget
come up with	contract	data	department	handout
introduce	job hunting	meeting	presentation	profit
proposal	realize	sales representative	urgent	vending machine

🎧 72　　A　　B

1. _____ _____
2. _____ _____
3. _____ _____
4. _____ _____
5. _____ _____
6. _____ _____
7. _____ _____
8. _____ _____
9. _____ _____
10. _____ _____

🎧 73　　A　　B

11. _____ _____
12. _____ _____
13. _____ _____
14. _____ _____
15. _____ _____
16. _____ _____
17. _____ _____
18. _____ _____
19. _____ _____
20. _____ _____

2　もう一度音声を聞き、1〜20の語句の意味を下の枠内から選んでB欄に書きましょう。

営業担当者	会議	会議事項	緊急の	契約
自動販売機	就職活動	提案	データ	導入する
〜に反対して	〜に申し込む	配布資料	部署	プレゼンテーション
約束	予算	利益	理解する	〜を思いつく

Listening Section

🔑 Key Point [Part 3] 設問パターンを知り、注意点を予測しておこう！

Part 3でよく出題される設問パターンがあります。

M: Hello. I'm Peter Smith, a sales representative for CGL Software. I have an appointment with Mr. Brown at 10 a.m.

W: I'm sorry, Mr. Smith, but he is in an urgent meeting now. It'll be finished in ten minutes.

M: Can I wait here in the lobby?

W: Sure. I'll get some coffee for you.

① 話者がどういう人物であるかを問う設問
Who most likely is the man?

② 会話の場所・場面を問う設問
Where is this conversation most likely taking place?

③ 会話のあとに起こる行動を推測させる設問
What will the woman do next?

🔊 Try 1　次のタスクに取り組みましょう。

1 2人の会話を聞き、設問の答えとして最も適切なものを選びましょう。　🎧 74

1. Where is this conversation most likely taking place?
   (A) At a waiting room
   (B) In a shop
   (C) At a meeting room

2. What will the woman probably do next?
   (A) Explain some data
   (B) Make a copy
   (C) Go to the vending machine

2 もう一度音声を聞き、＿＿部分を埋めましょう。そして、1の答えを確認しましょう。　🎧 74

M: Let's begin our ＿＿＿＿ ＿＿＿＿. The first ＿＿＿＿ item is whether to ＿＿＿＿ a new ＿＿＿＿ on the second floor.

W: I think it's a ＿＿＿＿ ＿＿＿＿. We need a new one.

M: Really? Cathy, you were ＿＿＿＿ the ＿＿＿＿, weren't you?

W: Yes. But the old ＿＿＿＿ often ＿＿＿＿ ＿＿＿＿ and it uses a lot of ink. Here is ＿＿＿＿ on how many ink refills we use every month. Please ＿＿＿＿ ＿＿＿＿ the ＿＿＿＿.

Try 2

音声を聞き、____部分を埋めましょう。 🎧 75

1. I'm _____. I was _____ _____ the _____.
2. We couldn't _____ _____ _____ any good idea in the _____.
3. Our _____ _____ _____ the _____.
4. _____ _____ the _____ _____ _____ _____.

Try 3

2人の会話を聞き、設問の答えとして最も適切なものを選びましょう。 🎧 76

Presentation schedule	Presenter
9:00 – 9:30	Hugo
9:30 – 10:00	Micheal
10:00 – 10:30	Linda
10:30 – 11:00	Jane
11:00 – 11:30	Mary

1. Who most likely are the speakers?
   (A) Colleagues
   (B) A couple
   (C) A teacher and a student
   (D) Friends
   Ⓐ Ⓑ Ⓒ Ⓓ

2. What will the woman do in the meeting?
   (A) She will agree with her boss.
   (B) She will introduce her idea.
   (C) She will propose a budget.
   (D) She will make an agenda.
   Ⓐ Ⓑ Ⓒ Ⓓ

3. Look at the graphic. Who will probably switch his or her presentation time with Jane?
   (A) Hugo
   (B) Michael
   (C) Linda
   (D) Mary
   Ⓐ Ⓑ Ⓒ Ⓓ

Active Reading 🎧 77

目標：____秒　1回目：____秒　2回目：____秒

Be a Better Presenter

There are four points to be a great presenter: understanding your audience, preparing your content, speaking confidently, and controlling your environment. Try the following to help you get all four. You have to find out who your audience is and what they want to learn from you. You have to prepare the information you are going to present in a way that the audience would find easy to understand. Make sure you start and end your presentation strongly. Practice your presentation before you give it.

語注　prepare 準備する　content 内容　confidently 自信をもって　make sure 必ず〜する

◆ 以下の説明が上の文章に合っていればT、間違っていればFを[　]に書きましょう。Fの場合は訂正しましょう。

1. [　] プレゼンテーションをするときは、聞き手がどのような人たちかを把握しておくほうがよい。
2. [　] プレゼンテーションの開始時と終了時には遠慮がちに話すほうがよい。

Reading Section

Key Point [Part 5 & 6] 仮定法

仮定法とは「願望」や「あり得ない」ことを述べる表現方法です。

仮定と条件の違い

仮定	事実に反するあり得ないこと	if I were a prince, (もし、私が王子なら)
条件	あるかもしれない単なる条件	if I have a day off tomorrow, (もし明日、休みなら)

仮定法の種類

現在を仮定する	仮定法過去
過去を仮定する	仮定法過去完了

仮定法の作り方

仮定法過去	<if+主語+過去形>, 主語+ would/could/should/might +動詞の原形
	If she **learned** how to use a computer, she <u>could find</u> a job. (もし彼女がコンピュータの使い方を学べば、仕事が見つかるのに。)
仮定法過去完了	<if+主語+過去完了形>, 主語+ would/could/should/might + have +過去分詞
	If I **had known** about the meeting, I <u>would have attended</u> it. (もしその会議について知っていたら、私はそれに出席したのに。)

仮定法の慣用表現

I wish 仮定法過去	…(主語)が〜すればいいなあ
I wish 仮定法過去完了	…(主語)が〜していたらよかったのに
If it were not for 〜	〜がなければ
as if 仮定法過去	まるで…(主語)が〜するかのように
as if 仮定法過去完了	まるで…(主語)が〜したかのように

Try 1 次の英文の空所に入る最も適切な語句を選びましょう。

If I were the president, I ------- a branch in London.

(A) will open
(B) have opened
(C) would open
(D) would have opened

HINT "If I were the president," は仮定法過去の if 節です。
(訳) もし、私が社長ならロンドンに支店を作るのに。

Think / Write / Share

ペアまたはグループで協力してやりましょう。

A あり得ないことを日本語で挙げてみましょう。

（例）妖精の王国へ行く／他界した祖父がまだ生きていたら

(　　)

B あり得ないことで、そうなったらいいなあと思うことについて、I wish を使って文をつくりましょう。

（例）I wish that I could go to the fairy kingdom. / I wish that my grandfather were still alive.

I wish (that) ＿＿＿＿＿＿＿＿＿＿＿＿＿＿＿＿＿＿＿＿＿＿＿＿＿＿＿＿＿＿＿＿＿＿

C アラジンの魔法のランプが願いを聞いてくれます。願いを仮定法過去の文で書きましょう。

（例）If I were a billionaire, I could buy three mansions.

＿＿

D タイムマシンに乗って過去に行けます。変えたい過去を仮定法過去完了の文で書きましょう。

（例）If I had studied harder, I could have passed the exam.

＿＿

E B～Dでつくった文をシェアしましょう。

Try 2 英文の空所に入る最も適切な語句を選びましょう。

1. She speaks as if she ------- my boss.
 (A) has been
 (B) were
 (C) am

2. If I were qualified, I ------- for the job.
 (A) applying
 (B) would apply
 (C) will apply

3. If I hadn't gotten sick, I ------- a deadline.
 (A) could have met
 (B) can meet
 (C) have met

4. I could have gotten a contract if I ------- a better presentation.
 (A) will give
 (B) have given
 (C) had given

5. I wish I ------- the importance of job hunting earlier.
   (A) had realized
   (B) realize
   (C) realizing

6. I would not have applied for the position if I ------- that.
   (A) have known
   (B) had known
   (C) knew

Try 3
英文の空所に入る最も適切な語句を選びましょう。

1. If sales department had succeeded, we ------- our profit by 10 percent last year.
   (A) will increase
   (B) been increasing
   (C) should increase
   (D) should have increased

2. If we ------- the annual meeting, I could have proposed this agenda.
   (A) will have
   (B) had
   (C) have had
   (D) had had

3. If Bill had been more careful, he ------- a serious error.
   (A) is making
   (B) won't be made
   (C) have made
   (D) wouldn't have made

4. He talks at the meeting as if he ------- everything.
   (A) knew
   (B) known
   (C) had known
   (D) have known

5. If it had not been for my support, he ------- resigned.
   (A) might
   (B) might have
   (C) might have had to
   (D) might have been

6. If he ------- his safety belt, he wouldn't have been injured.
   (A) had been wearing
   (B) have been wearing
   (C) have worn
   (D) is wearing

Unit 12 News

関係代名詞

Vocabulary

1 1〜20の語句を聞き取り、下の枠内から選んでA欄に書きましょう。

accident	block	broadcast	clearly	construction
degree	discovery	downtown	due to	happen
latest	news reporter	search	survive	temperature
traffic	traffic jam	update	vehicle	weather

🎧 78   A   B

1. _____ _____
2. _____ _____
3. _____ _____
4. _____ _____
5. _____ _____
6. _____ _____
7. _____ _____
8. _____ _____
9. _____ _____
10. _____ _____

🎧 79   A   B

11. _____ _____
12. _____ _____
13. _____ _____
14. _____ _____
15. _____ _____
16. _____ _____
17. _____ _____
18. _____ _____
19. _____ _____
20. _____ _____

2 もう一度音声を聞き、1〜20の語句の意味を下の枠内から選んでB欄に書きましょう。

生き残る	起きる	温度	車	建設
交通	交通渋滞	最新情報	最新の	探す
事故	中心街へ	天気	度	〜のせいで
はっきりと	発見	閉鎖する	放送する	報道記者

Listening Section

🗝 Key Point ［Part 4］ キーワードから説明文の種類と大意をつかもう！

Part 4 では、まとまった量の英文が一気に読み上げられるので、キーワードを聞き取り、説明文の種類と大まかな内容をつかむ必要があります。種類（アナウンス、ニュース、広告、留守番メッセージ、ガイドツアー、スピーチなど）については、冒頭の指示文（Questions 71 through 73 refer to the following announcement/report/speech.）がヒントになることがあるので、最初から注意して聞きましょう。

交通情報に関するニュースの場合のキーワード

Now we give you a traffic information update. Police have closed Highway 80 and 101 due to ice on the road. Conditions are dangerous for driving. It's snowing now and you can't see clearly. Please be careful. We'll bring you more traffic information at 10:00. And now back to the sport highlights.

traffic information「交通情報」　Highway 80 and 101「ハイウェイ 80 号線と 101 号線」　ice on the road「路上の氷」
condition「状態」　dangerous「危険な」　can't see clearly「はっきりと見えない」

🔊 Try 1　次のタスクに取り組みましょう。

1 説明文を聞き、設問の答えとして最も適切なものを選びましょう。　🎧 80

1. What kind of announcement is this?
   (A) An announcement at an airport
   (B) A weather report
   (C) A recorded message

2. What will happen over the weekend?
   (A) It will be sunny and warm.
   (B) It will be rainy.
   (C) It will be sunny but cold.

2 もう一度音声を聞き、＿＿部分を埋めましょう。そして、1の答えを確認しましょう。　🎧 80

Good morning. This is Robert Smith with today's ＿＿＿＿＿ ＿＿＿＿＿. There's ＿＿＿＿＿ ＿＿＿＿＿ today from yesterday. It'll ＿＿＿＿＿ and it'll be ＿＿＿＿＿ ＿＿＿＿＿. ＿＿＿＿＿ will be around 3 degrees. However, the good news is that it'll be ＿＿＿＿＿ and ＿＿＿＿＿ over the ＿＿＿＿＿. No worries about rain. ＿＿＿＿＿ ＿＿＿＿＿ ＿＿＿＿＿ cycling with the family or washing your car. ＿＿＿＿＿ ＿＿＿＿＿. You'll hear major news items next.

Try 2   音声を聞き、____部分を埋めましょう。   🎧 81

1. Next is _____ _____ _____ _____.

2. The _____ will be _____ _____ _____.

3. _____ _____ _____ is causing a _____ _____.

4. The main _____ is _____ _____ _____ _____ on the road.

Try 3   説明文を聞き、設問の答えとして最も適切なものを選びましょう。   🎧 82

1. What kind of announcement is this?
   (A) A weather report
   (B) An advertisement for a new car
   (C) A traffic report
   (D) A speech at a contest
   　　　　　　　　　　Ⓐ Ⓑ Ⓒ Ⓓ

2. What does the speaker advise drivers to do when going to San Francisco?
   (A) Take another road
   (B) Look at signals
   (C) Go south
   (D) Drive slowly
   　　　　　　　　　　Ⓐ Ⓑ Ⓒ Ⓓ

3. What will drivers run into if they are driving downtown on Highway 2?
   (A) Road construction
   (B) Heavy rain
   (C) Icy road
   (D) A traffic jam
   　　　　　　　　　　Ⓐ Ⓑ Ⓒ Ⓓ

Active Reading   🎧 83

目標：____秒　1回目：____秒　2回目：____秒

Weather Reports

In the past, inaccurate reports on weather disasters affected many people and cost a lot of lives and money. However, scientists today say that because of new technology, weather reporting has become more advanced and correct. They can now predict extreme weather up to seven days in advance. Not only are the warnings of extreme weather conditions made earlier, but they are also more correct. Instruments can catch changes in the weather that were invisible in the past. Currently, scientists say that weather reporting is only 70% accurate, but they are working hard to make sure they get closer to being 100% accurate.

語注　inaccurate 不正確な　disaster 災害　affect 影響を与える　predict 予測する　extreme 極端な

◆ 上の文章の内容に合うように、以下の空所を埋めましょう。

(1.　　　　　　　) のおかげで天気予報は進歩し、現在の天気予報の的中率は (2.　　　　　　　) ％である。

Reading Section

🔑 Key Point [Part 5 & 6] 関係代名詞

関係代名詞の後ろに何かが欠けている不完全な節を続けて、先行詞を説明・修飾します。

関係代名詞の種類

先行詞	主格	目的格	所有格
人	who	who / whom	whose
人以外	which	which	whose
人と物の両方	that	that	

主格 節に欠けているもの：主語

I know **a man** who (*) is a news reporter.（私は報道記者の男性を知っている。）

　　　　↓
　　A man is a news reporter.（ * ）に当てはまる a man が先行詞

目的格 節に欠けているもの：目的語

The news which we watched (*) on TV was shocking.

（テレビで見たニュースはショッキングだった。）

　　　　↓
　　We watched **the news** on TV.（ * ）に当てはまる the news が先行詞

所有格 節に欠けているもの：所有格

I know **a girl** whose (*) mother is a weather forecaster.

（私はお母さんが気象予報士の女の子を知っている。）

　　　　↓
　　A girl's mother is a weather forecaster.（ * ）に当てはまる a girl が先行詞
　　(Her)

📖 **Try 1**　次の英文の空所に入る最も適切な語句を選びましょう。

There is a traffic jam because of an accident ------- happened three hours ago.

(A) who
(B) which
(C) whom
(D) whose

HINT 💡　happened の主語に当たるものは何でしょうか。
（訳）3時間前に起きた事故のせいで渋滞している。

Think / Write / Share

ペアまたはグループで協力してやりましょう。

Q 自分にとって理想の相手はどんな人でしょうか。書き出しに合わせて文をつくり、シェアしましょう。

1. (例) I want a boyfriend who is rich.

    I want a boyfriend/girlfriend who _____.

2. (例) I want a girlfriend whose hair is black.

    I want a boyfriend/girlfriend whose _____.

3. (例) I want a boyfriend whom I have a dream with.

    I want a boyfriend/girlfriend whom _____.

Try 2 　英文の空所に入る最も適切な語句を選びましょう。

1. There are many gray clouds ------- will bring rain.
   (A) whose
   (B) who
   (C) which

2. This is the hottest summer ------- we have had in 20 years.
   (A) whom
   (B) that
   (C) who

3. Production couldn't keep up with the needs ------- consumers have.
   (A) who
   (B) whom
   (C) which

4. The driver ------- the police caught on the highway was fined.
   (A) whom
   (B) whose
   (C) which

5. The latest news ------- we heard on the radio was wrong.
   (A) who
   (B) which
   (C) whom

6. He is the Nobel Prize winner ------- discovery was broadcast all over the world.
   (A) whose
   (B) that
   (C) who

Key Point [Part 7] キーワードからトピックをすばやくつかもう！

長文の量に負けないために、まずはキーワードをキャッチして、すばやくトピックを把握しましょう。トピックをつかめれば、内容を理解するスピードは格段に上がります。

次の文書にはキーワードが網掛けで示されています。キーワードに目を通して、この文書が何について書かれているかを大まかにイメージしてみましょう。

Monday day:	Cloudy with rain later. High temperature of 12 ℃.
Monday night:	Rain and fog. Low temperature of 6 ℃.
Tuesday:	Rain continuing. Strong winds with temperatures approaching 10 ℃.
Wednesday:	Clearing early. Partly sunny and warmer with temperature near 15 ℃.

この文書は「天気」に関するものだと判断できるので、天候に関する設問が予想されます。また、広告や案内文などはタイトルや見出し、表などにも注目すると、トピックをつかみやすくなります。

Try 1　上の文書を読んで、設問の答えとして最も適切なものを選びましょう。

1. What temperature is predicted for Monday night?
   (A) 6 ℃
   (B) 10 ℃
   (C) 12 ℃
   (D) 15 ℃

HINT　月曜の夜の情報を探してみましょう。

2. What is this information about?
   (A) A weekly schedule
   (B) The weather
   (C) Sales figures
   (D) Record temperatures

HINT　トピックを考えてみましょう。

Try 2

文章をすばやく読みながらキーワードを囲み、それぞれのトピックとして最も適切なものを選びましょう。

(A) 会議日程の変更　　(C) 工場の閉鎖　　(E) 新製品
(B) サッカーW杯優勝　(D) 巨大竜巻　　　(F) ノーベル平和賞

1. _____

Rainbow Factory is one of the nation's largest companies which produce healthy food. Next month, we will introduce our new "Speedy Success" that uses only fresh ingredients from local farms. We will offer our "Speedy Success" at many supermarkets and department stores, so you can easily try our new "Speedy Success."

2. _____

Germany and Argentina played in the final of the World Cup in Brazil on July 13. Germany had Magnus, who scored the only goal of the game in the second half of overtime. As a result, Germany beat Argentina 1-0 and won the World Cup for the first time in 24 years.

3. _____

Sophia, the 17-year-old girl from Switzerland who survived the attack, became the youngest Nobel Peace Prize winner on Friday for working to promote girls' education.

4. _____

Rescuers are searching for the people who were left after a huge tornado hit Oklahoma City in the southern United States on Monday, flattening homes and crushing at least two elementary schools.

Try 3 文書を読んで、3つの設問の答えとして最も適切なものを選びましょう。

Centerville Intermediate School Newsletter

The survey was conducted by board members to improve school facilities.

Question of the month: What is your favorite place at school?

Student response:

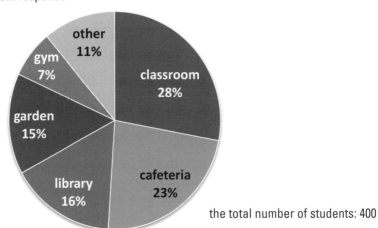

the total number of students: 400

1. What is the purpose of this survey?
   (A) To develop the school's facilities
   (B) To provide advice
   (C) To introduce a new classroom
   (D) To offer an invitation

   Ⓐ Ⓑ Ⓒ Ⓓ

2. What is the most popular place?
   (A) The cafeteria
   (B) Classrooms
   (C) The garden
   (D) The library

   Ⓐ Ⓑ Ⓒ Ⓓ

3. How many students like to be in the garden?
   (A) 30
   (B) 40
   (C) 50
   (D) 60

   Ⓐ Ⓑ Ⓒ Ⓓ

Unit 13 Ads

関係副詞

Vocabulary

1 1〜20の語句を聞き取り、下の枠内から選んでA欄に書きましょう。

advantage	advertisement	appeal	attach	candidate
celebration	customer	details	for free	headline
magazine	mention	newspaper	product	quality
remodel	résumé	successful	warrant	website

🎧 84   A   B   🎧 85   A   B

1. _____ _____   11. _____ _____
2. _____ _____   12. _____ _____
3. _____ _____   13. _____ _____
4. _____ _____   14. _____ _____
5. _____ _____   15. _____ _____
6. _____ _____   16. _____ _____
7. _____ _____   17. _____ _____
8. _____ _____   18. _____ _____
9. _____ _____   19. _____ _____
10. _____ _____   20. _____ _____

2 もう一度音声を聞き、1〜20の語句の意味を下の枠内から選んでB欄に書きましょう。

ウェブサイト	改装する	興味を引く	言及する	広告
候補者	顧客	雑誌	質	祝典
詳細	新聞	成功した	製品	強み
添付する	保証する	見出し	無料で	履歴書

Listening Section

Key Point [Part 4] 設問の中の具体的な語句に注目しよう！

Part 4は、3つの設問の中に説明文の内容を推測できるような具体的な語句が出ていることが多くあります。

This is a beautiful leather bag made in France. The leather is really good and goes with any outfits. We offer it to you for only $100, not our usual price of $200. The leather is from Italy, so we can warrant its quality. Touch and feel the great quality. If you call us within the next two hours, you can get the special price on TV Shopper. Call us now at 007-8855-3241.

1. What is the price of the bag in the advertisement?
2. Where is the leather from?
3. How can viewers and listeners get the special price?

Try 1 次のタスクに取り組みましょう。

1 店のコマーシャルを聞き、設問の答えとして最も適切なものを選びましょう。 🎧 86

1. What does Auto ABC offer its customers?
   (A) Free maintenance
   (B) Free maps of the town
   (C) New cars

2. What is mentioned about Auto ABC's business days?
   (A) They are closed on Sunday.
   (B) They are closed on Monday.
   (C) They are open on weekdays.

2 もう一度音声を聞き、＿＿部分を埋めましょう。そして、1の答えを確認しましょう。 🎧 86

If you're looking for a ＿＿＿＿＿ ＿＿＿＿＿, come to Auto ABC this weekend. We're selling cars at unbelievable ＿＿＿＿＿. We have various cars, compacts, family vans, hybrids, and ＿＿＿＿＿. All of our ＿＿＿＿＿ are given ＿＿＿＿＿ ＿＿＿＿＿ every six months. We're ＿＿＿＿＿ from ＿＿＿＿＿ to ＿＿＿＿＿, ＿＿＿＿＿ a.m. to ＿＿＿＿＿ p.m. Come and see us on Washington Street.

Try 2 音声を聞き、＿＿部分を埋めましょう。 🎧 87

1. We will offer a ＿＿＿＿＿ ＿＿＿＿＿ next ＿＿＿＿＿.
2. ＿＿＿＿＿ can get a ＿＿＿＿＿ ＿＿＿＿＿ for items.
3. The ＿＿＿＿＿ ＿＿＿＿＿ you ＿＿＿＿＿ ＿＿＿＿＿.
4. For ＿＿＿＿＿ ＿＿＿＿＿, ＿＿＿＿＿ ＿＿＿＿＿ ＿＿＿＿＿ ＿＿＿＿＿ ＿＿＿＿＿.

Try 3 　説明文を聞き、設問の答えとして最も適切なものを選びましょう。

Reopening Special Events	
Program	Time
Design festival	10:00 a.m. Saturday
Storytelling	2:00 p.m. Saturday
Puppet show	11:00 a.m. Sunday
Gospel show	3:00 p.m. Sunday

1. Who will be invited to the celebration as a guest?
   (A) A musician
   (B) A radio personality
   (C) An actor
   (D) A child
   Ⓐ Ⓑ Ⓒ Ⓓ

2. How long will the events last?
   (A) One day
   (B) Two days
   (C) Two weeks
   (D) One month
   Ⓐ Ⓑ Ⓒ Ⓓ

3. Look at the graphic. What will be the final event?
   (A) Design festival
   (B) Storytelling
   (C) Puppet show
   (D) Gospel show
   Ⓐ Ⓑ Ⓒ Ⓓ

Active Reading　🎧 89

目標：＿＿＿秒　1回目：＿＿＿秒　2回目：＿＿＿秒

Ad Strategies

Every copywriter should know the four common ad strategies to make people more aware of a product and raise sales. One strategy is called "Before and After": showing that the negative situation before having the product will be erased by getting it. Another is called "Advice": suggesting an action that is related to the product (e.g., getting more calcium for healthier bones by drinking more of the milk you are selling). The third is called "Empathy": making people emotionally connected to a cause the company supports. The fourth is called "Testimonial": having an outside person (usually a celebrity) to promote the product.

語注　strategy 戦略　product 製品　erase 消す　suggest 示唆する　emotionally 感情的に

◆ コピーライターが行う次の戦略の名称を上の文章から抜き出しましょう。

1. 有名人にその製品を推奨してもらう戦略：＿＿＿＿＿＿＿＿＿＿＿＿＿＿＿＿

2. その製品を使うことにより、悪いことが取り除かれたと伝える戦略：＿＿＿＿＿＿＿＿＿＿＿＿＿＿＿＿

Reading Section

🔑 Key Point ［Part 5 & 6］ 関係副詞

関係副詞は何も欠けていない完全な節（各例文の下線部）を導きます。

関係副詞の種類

先行詞	場所	時	理由	方法
関係副詞	where	when	why	how

関係副詞は＜前置詞＋関係代名詞＞を使って言い換えることができます。

where	This is the shop **where** (= at which) <u>we can buy anything</u>.
	（これが私たちが何でも買えるお店です。）
when	I'm looking forward to the day **when** (= on which) <u>you visit us</u>.
	（お越しになる日を楽しみにしています。）
why	I'm telling you the reason **why** (= for which) <u>we should choose it</u>.
	（私たちがそれを選ぶべき理由をお話しします。）
how	I'll show you **how** (= the way in which) <u>we can get it</u>.
	（どのようにしてそれを入手できるかをお教えします。）

省略可能な先行詞

the time, the place, the reason などの先行詞は、よく省略されます。

関係代名詞と関係副詞の見分け方

関係詞の後ろが「何も欠けていない完全な節」かどうかを確認します。次の英文の下線部をチェックして、（　）に入る関係詞を考えてみましょう。

1. This is the house (　　　) <u>my mother lives</u>.
2. This is the house (　　　) <u>my mother lives in</u>.
3. This is the house in (　　　) <u>my mother lives</u>.

📖 Try 1　次の英文の空所に入る最も適切な語を選びましょう。

His sense for graphic art is the reason ------- he got an award.

(A) who
(B) what
(C) where
(D) why

HINT 空所の後ろは完全な文、前にはthe reasonがあります。
（訳）グラフィックアートのセンスが彼の受賞の理由だ。

Think / Write / Share

ペアまたはグループで協力してやりましょう。

Q 2つの文が同じ意味になるように空所を埋めましょう。

1. Canada is a country _____ I want to live.

   Canada is a country _____ _____ I want to live.

   (カナダは、私が住みたい国です。)

2. This is the city _____ she was born.

   This is the city _____ _____ she was born.

   (これは、彼女が生まれた街です。)

3. The day _____ I will start is next Friday.

   The day _____ _____ I will start is next Friday.

   (私が始めるのは、次の金曜日です。)

Try 2
英文の空所に入る最も適切な語句を選びましょう。

1. This is the magazine ------- we can see our company's ad.
   (A) who
   (B) which
   (C) where
   Ⓐ Ⓑ Ⓒ

2. I'll tell you ------- you can make a good presentation.
   (A) how
   (B) which
   (C) that
   Ⓐ Ⓑ Ⓒ

3. The catch phrase is the place ------- you can explain your product.
   (A) when
   (B) where
   (C) why
   Ⓐ Ⓑ Ⓒ

4. The reason ------- we need a good headline is to appeal to readers.
   (A) why
   (B) when
   (C) where
   Ⓐ Ⓑ Ⓒ

Unit 13 Ads　関係副詞

Key Point [Part 7] マルチ（ダブル）パッセージでは情報を照らし合わせよう！

意外に点数を稼げるダブルパッセージ（マルチパッセージ）は、設問のヒントが1つのパッセージにあるのか、または複数のパッセージにあるのかを見極めることが大切です。

①広告

Enjoy Ice Cream Every Single Day

Buy one vanilla ice cream
Get one small ice cream free
Monday and Thursday

Buy one chocolate ice cream
Get one small ice cream free
Tuesday and Friday

Lucky's Ice Cream
Open 7 days a week
11 a.m. to 8 p.m.

Free drink
with purchase of large ice cream
Wednesday only

Buy one Lucky's Ice Cream
Get 1/2 off another ice cream
Saturday and Sunday

②メール

From:	Emily Wilton
To:	Nancy Cooper
Date:	November 12
Subject:	After lunch

Hi Nancy,

I'm looking forward to seeing you tomorrow. I was thinking about the meeting place and found a nice ad. How about meeting at the Lucky's Ice Cream shop? I love coffee and you love ice cream, so tomorrow is the best day for us! I'll be there around 2 p.m.

See you then!

Emily

Try 1

左の2つの文書に関して、次の設問文を訳しましょう。そして、①、②、③「両方」のうち、どの内容について問われているかを考え、（ ）に数字を記入して答えましょう。

1. What is being advertised?

   訳：_____ （　）

2. What time does the shop open?

   訳：_____ （　）

3. What can customers get for free on Wednesday if they buy a large ice cream?

   訳：_____ （　）

4. What day is November 12?

   訳：_____ （　）

5. What will happen at 2 p.m. on November 13?

   訳：_____ （　）

Try 2

左の2つの文書を読んで、Try 1の5つの設問の答えとして最も適切なものを選びましょう。

1. (A) A shoe shop
   (B) A bag shop
   (C) An ice cream shop
   (D) A cookie shop
   Ⓐ Ⓑ Ⓒ Ⓓ

2. (A) 11 a.m.
   (B) 8 p.m.
   (C) 9 p.m.
   (D) 11 p.m.
   Ⓐ Ⓑ Ⓒ Ⓓ

3. (A) A beverage
   (B) An ice cream
   (C) Some vanilla
   (D) Some chocolate
   Ⓐ Ⓑ Ⓒ Ⓓ

4. (A) Monday
   (B) Tuesday
   (C) Wednesday
   (D) Sunday
   Ⓐ Ⓑ Ⓒ Ⓓ

5. (A) Friends will meet.
   (B) A presentation will be made.
   (C) Gifts will be bought.
   (D) Someone will run in the park.
   Ⓐ Ⓑ Ⓒ Ⓓ

 **Try 3**　2つの文書を読んで、5つの設問の答えとして最も適切なものを選びましょう。

Translator
Wanted

Smith Inc. in Washington is looking to add a responsible, hardworking person to our company.

Qualified candidates should have:
○ Fluent Spanish
○ Business experience

Our benefits:
○ Above-average pay
○ Paid holidays
○ Health insurance

Send your résumé to: James Mack (jamesmk@hr.smith-wgt.com) of Human Resources

---

From:　　Carlos Ronald
To:　　　James Mack
Date:　　January 15
Subject:　Translator position

Dear Mr. Mack:

I am interested in the position of translator advertised in today's *Daily News*. My résumé is attached.

Last May, I completed my degree in TESOL at Park College, and since then I have been working in the international department of Green Industries.

My first language is Spanish, but I have studied English and am fluent in this language. I look forward to hearing from you.

Best regards,
Carlos Ronald

1. What is Smith Inc. looking for?
   (A) A teacher
   (B) A customer
   (C) A translator
   (D) A clerk

2. What is offered to the successful candidate?
   (A) Good pay
   (B) A chance to travel
   (C) A training session
   (D) Promotion to manager

3. What is the purpose of the e-mail?
   (A) To present a job description
   (B) To say hello
   (C) To express interest in a job opportunity
   (D) To apply for Internet banking

4. When is the ad in the newspaper?
   (A) January 15
   (B) January 16
   (C) February 15
   (D) February 16

5. What is Mr. Ronald's advantage for this position?
   (A) A sociable personality
   (B) Excellent leadership
   (C) Computer skills
   (D) His language ability

Post-test (問題の音声は教師用 CD に収録されています)

LISTENING TEST

In the Listening test, you will be asked to demonstrate how well you understand spoken English. The entire Listening test will last approximately 12 minutes. There are four parts, and directions are given for each part. You must mark your answers on the separate answer sheet. Do not write your answers in your test book.

PART 1

Directions: For each question in this part, you will hear four statements about a picture in your test book. When you hear the statements, you must select the one statement that best describes what you see in the picture. Then find the number of the question on your answer sheet and mark your answer. The statements will not be printed in your test book and will be spoken only one time.

Example

Sample Answer

Statement (C), "They're sitting at a table," is the best description of the picture, so you should select answer (C) and mark it on your answer sheet.

1.

Ⓐ Ⓑ Ⓒ Ⓓ

2.

Ⓐ Ⓑ Ⓒ Ⓓ

GO ON TO THE NEXT PAGE

PART 2

Directions: You will hear a question or statement and three responses spoken in English. They will not be printed in your test book and will be spoken only one time. Select the best response to the question or statement and mark the letter (A), (B), or (C) on your answer sheet.

3. Ⓐ Ⓑ Ⓒ
4. Ⓐ Ⓑ Ⓒ
5. Ⓐ Ⓑ Ⓒ
6. Ⓐ Ⓑ Ⓒ
7. Ⓐ Ⓑ Ⓒ
8. Ⓐ Ⓑ Ⓒ

PART 3

Directions: You will hear some conversations between two or more people. You will be asked to answer three questions about what the speakers say in each conversation. Select the best response to each question and mark the letter (A), (B), (C), or (D) on your answer sheet. The conversations will not be printed in your test book and will be spoken only one time.

9. Who most likely are the speakers?
   (A) Customers
   (B) Shop clerks
   (C) Teachers
   (D) Colleagues
   Ⓐ Ⓑ Ⓒ Ⓓ

10. Why does the woman say, "Why not"?
    (A) She will go and see her boss.
    (B) She likes Tom's presentation.
    (C) She will propose her idea.
    (D) She is easy to talk to.
    Ⓐ Ⓑ Ⓒ Ⓓ

11. What will the woman probably do next?
    (A) She will go home.
    (B) She will meet her boss.
    (C) She will make a presentation.
    (D) She will join a meeting.

12. Where is this conversation most likely taking place?
    (A) In a shop
    (B) In a school
    (C) In a hospital
    (D) In a gym
    Ⓐ Ⓑ Ⓒ Ⓓ

13. What does the woman say about the T-shirts?
    (A) They're made of cotton.
    (B) They're on sale today.
    (C) They're good for kids.
    (D) They come in one color.
    Ⓐ Ⓑ Ⓒ Ⓓ

14. What does the man want to do with his purchase?
    (A) Give it as a gift
    (B) Use it soon
    (C) Return it
    (D) Exchange it for a different design
    Ⓐ Ⓑ Ⓒ Ⓓ

15. What is the conversation mainly about?
    (A) Arranging the date of the appointment
    (B) Their boss
    (C) Going on a business trip
    (D) Free time
    Ⓐ Ⓑ Ⓒ Ⓓ

16. What does one of the speakers imply about his or her boss?
    (A) He is busy.
    (B) He is tired.
    (C) He is talkative.
    (D) He is nice.
    Ⓐ Ⓑ Ⓒ Ⓓ

17. When will they meet?
    (A) On Monday
    (B) On Wednesday
    (C) On Thursday
    (D) On Friday
    Ⓐ Ⓑ Ⓒ Ⓓ

GO ON TO THE NEXT PAGE

PART 4

Directions: You will hear some talks given by a single speaker. You will be asked to answer three questions about what the speaker says in each talk. Select the best response to each question and mark the letter (A), (B), (C), or (D) on your answer sheet. The talks will not be printed in your test book and will be spoken only one time.

18. What does the speaker say about tonight's weather?
    (A) It will rain and be cold.
    (B) It will snow a lot.
    (C) It will rain after 5 p.m.
    (D) It will be mostly clear.

19. What should listeners be careful about tomorrow?
    (A) Cold temperatures
    (B) Heavy rain
    (C) Icy roads
    (D) Snow

20. When will it probably stop snowing?
    (A) Tuesday
    (B) Wednesday
    (C) Thursday
    (D) Friday

21. What kind of goods will NOT be discounted?
    (A) Boots
    (B) Accessories
    (C) Clothes
    (D) Bags

22. How long will the clearance sale last?
    (A) One day
    (B) Five days
    (C) A week
    (D) A month

23. What can shoppers take advantage of at the register?
    (A) Getting a coupon for free meal
    (B) Having beverages
    (C) Getting another 40 percent discount
    (D) Winning free tickets

READING TEST

In the Reading test, you will read a variety of texts and answer several different types of reading comprehension questions. The entire Reading test will last 20 minutes. There are three parts, and directions are given for each part. You are encouraged to answer as many questions as possible within the time allowed.

You must mark your answers on the separate answer sheet. Do not write your answers in your test book.

PART 5

Directions: A word or phrase is missing in each of the sentences below. Four answer choices are given below each sentence. Select the best answer to complete the sentence. Then mark the letter (A), (B), (C), or (D) on your answer sheet.

24. To ------- high-quality vegetables, a good environment is needed.
    (A) produce
    (B) product
    (C) productive
    (D) productively
    Ⓐ Ⓑ Ⓒ Ⓓ

25. Mr. Parker ------- to see you since two o'clock.
    (A) waited
    (B) has been waiting
    (C) are waiting
    (D) will wait
    Ⓐ Ⓑ Ⓒ Ⓓ

26. George will participate ------- a seminar in London.
    (A) of
    (B) on
    (C) with
    (D) in
    Ⓐ Ⓑ Ⓒ Ⓓ

27. The man ------- repaired my computer is good at his job.
    (A) who
    (B) which
    (C) whose
    (D) whom
    Ⓐ Ⓑ Ⓒ Ⓓ

28. I have to ------- writing the report by tomorrow.
    (A) finish
    (B) agreed
    (C) hope
    (D) fail
    Ⓐ Ⓑ Ⓒ Ⓓ

29. The man ------- over there is my teacher.
    (A) stands
    (B) standing
    (C) stood
    (D) stand
    Ⓐ Ⓑ Ⓒ Ⓓ

GO ON TO THE NEXT PAGE

30. ------- the accident, all the flights have been canceled.
    (A) Because
    (B) Because of
    (C) If
    (D) Although

31. Please give me the reason ------- you didn't come to the meeting yesterday.
    (A) where
    (B) why
    (C) when
    (D) how

PART 6

Directions: Read the texts that follow. A word, phrase, or sentence is missing in parts of each text. Four answer choices for each question are given below the text. Select the best answer to complete the text. Then mark the letter (A), (B), (C), or (D) on your answer sheet.

Questions 32–35 refer to the following advertisement.

Carleton Hotel in California

Are you looking ---**32**.--- a good hotel in California? ---**33**.--- It is located very close to downtown and ---**34**.--- easy access to many famous tourist sites.

For more information, or if you would like to make a reservation, please visit ---**35**.--- website at www.ttt.sss.

32. (A) across
    (B) of
    (C) for
    (D) on

33. (A) Why don't you come to California?
    (B) Guests are asked to check out before 11 A.M.
    (C) We are fully booked this week.
    (D) Carleton Hotel is perfect for you!

34. (A) offering
    (B) offer
    (C) to offer
    (D) offers

35. (A) we
    (B) our
    (C) us
    (D) ours

PART 7

Directions: In this part you will read a selection of texts, such as magazine and newspaper articles, e-mails, and instant messages. Each text or set of texts is followed by several questions. Select the best answer for each question and mark the letter (A), (B), (C), or (D) on your answer sheet.

Questions 36–38 refer to the following information.

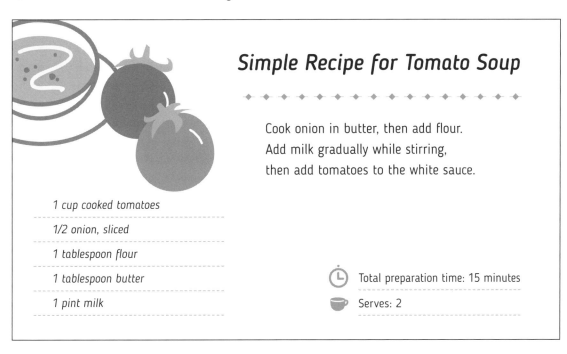

Simple Recipe for Tomato Soup

Cook onion in butter, then add flour.
Add milk gradually while stirring,
then add tomatoes to the white sauce.

1 cup cooked tomatoes
1/2 onion, sliced
1 tablespoon flour
1 tablespoon butter
1 pint milk

Total preparation time: 15 minutes
Serves: 2

36. Which of the following is NOT needed to make this soup?
(A) Vegetables
(B) Flour
(C) Cream
(D) Milk

37. According to the recipe, what is the final step?
(A) Cook the onion
(B) Add the flour
(C) Put in the tomatoes
(D) Stir the mixture

38. How many people is this tomato soup for?
(A) Two
(B) Four
(C) Six
(D) Eight

GO ON TO THE NEXT PAGE

Questions 39–41 refer to the following text message chain.

Gloria	12:58
I'm having trouble finding your building, Duncan. Sorry, I'll be late.	
Duncan	1:01
Where are you now?	
Gloria	1:01
I'm just next to West Bank.	
Duncan	1:02
We're located two blocks away.	
Gloria	1:03
OK, I'm heading that way.	
Duncan	1:04
Go straight and you'll see Organic Foods Supermarket on your left.	
Gloria	1:08
I see that.	
Duncan	1:09
That's it. Our building is just across the street. There's a sign at the entrance.	
Gloria	1:10
Great. I'll see you in a few minutes.	

39. What is suggested about Gloria?
    (A) She is lost.
    (B) She doesn't know Duncan.
    (C) She is giving directions.
    (D) She goes to West Bank.

40. At 1:09, what does Duncan mean when he writes, "That's it"?
    (A) Our house is close.
    (B) That's too bad.
    (C) Organic Foods Supermarket is good.
    (D) That's what you're supposed to see.

41. When was the appointment probably scheduled for?
    (A) At 12:00
    (B) At 12:30
    (C) At 12:58
    (D) At 1:00

Questions 42–45 refer to the following announcement.

Announcement

We are very sorry to announce the retirement of Mr. Sullivan who is a sales manager. —[1]— Mr. Sullivan has been one of our most reliable employees, giving us 40 years of loyal service. —[2]— We would like to invite you to an event on Sunday, December 15, commemorating Mr. Sullivan's time with us. —[3]— We plan to give him flowers after his speech. We hope that you will be able to join us in this celebration. —[4]—

Date: December 15
Time: 10:00 a.m.   Welcome drink service
         11:00 a.m.   Presentation by Mr. Sullivan
         12:00 p.m.   Luncheon at Wellington Hall
         3:00 p.m.   Photo session

42. What is the purpose of the announcement?
    (A) To request attendance at an event
    (B) To make an appointment for a party
    (C) To organize a vacation
    (D) To make plans for a business trip

43. The word "sorry" in line 1 is closest in meaning to
    (A) lucky
    (B) common
    (C) different
    (D) sad

44. What kind of people would be interested in attending this event?
    (A) Custormers
    (B) Teachers
    (C) Coworkers
    (D) Students

45. In which of the positions marked [1], [2], [3] and [4] does the following sentence best belong?

    "At the event, Mr. Sullivan will make a speech about the secret of success in business."

    (A) [1]
    (B) [2]
    (C) [3]
    (D) [4]

Questions 46–50 refer to the following invoice, e-mail and voucher.

FORESTS OFFICE SUPPLIES

Tel.: 289-467-8902

Invoice No.: 08-671-555

Bill to: Mr. John Scott

Description	Units	Unit Price	Amount
Baymax color printer	2	$199.99	$399.98
CNG copy paper	6	$24.99	$149.94
Lennox metal bookcases	3	$65.99	$197.97
Millar transparent tape	8	$3.99	$31.92
		Sub Total	$779.81
		Shipping	$20.00
		Total	$799.81

If you have any questions about this invoice, please contact Jennifer Fairbanks.

From: John Scott
To: fairbanks@forests.com
Date: Jan 25
Subject: Invoice error

Dear Ms. Fairbanks,

My name is John Scott, and I ordered some products from your online shop. I received the products and invoice, but there are some errors in the invoice.

I received two color printers and the invoice states that the amount is $399.98, but I used a voucher. I will attach it to this e-mail for confirmation. The amount of the Baymax color printer on the invoice is wrong.

Please check your records and correct the error as soon as possible.

Regards,
John Scott

46. How much was John Scott charged?
 (A) $399.98
 (B) $779.81
 (C) $20.00
 (D) $799.81

47. Who is most likely in charge of invoices at Forests Office Supplies?
 (A) John Scott
 (B) May Concern
 (C) Jennifer Fairbanks
 (D) Sandy Ridge

48. What is the main purpose of this e-mail?
 (A) To complain about some products
 (B) To order more goods
 (C) To report a mistake in an invoice
 (D) To point out a mistake in calculation

49. How much will the new invoice to charge?
 (A) $399.98
 (B) $599.82
 (C) $779.81
 (D) $799.81

50. What will John Scott send with this e-mail?
 (A) A voucher
 (B) A printer
 (C) An invoice
 (D) A copy paper

Appendix

人称代名詞の変化表 (→ p. 24)

単数形 / 複数形	主格 (〜は／が)	所有格 (〜の)	目的格 (〜を／に)	所有代名詞 (〜のもの)	再帰代名詞 (〜自身)
私	I	my	me	mine	myself
私たち	we	our	us	ours	ourselves
あなた	you	your	you	yours	yourself
あなたたち	you	your	you	yours	yourselves
彼	he	his	him	his	himself
彼ら	they	their	them	theirs	themselves
彼女	she	her	her	hers	herself
彼女たち	they	their	them	theirs	themselves
それ	it	its	it	—	itself
それら	they	their	them	theirs	themselves

Glossary

各ユニットのVocabularyで取り上げられている語句をアルファベット順にまとめました。番号は、各ユニット内のListening Section以降 (Tryのスクリプトなども含む) で初出の掲載ページを示しています。

A

absence	35
accident	90
accommodations	44
actor	65
advantage	103
advertisement	96
advise	72
against	82
agenda	82
aisle seat	47
amusement park	64
annual report	80
apologize	71
appeal	99
apply for	85
appointment	82
arrival time	47
attach	102
attend	38
audience	65
available	64
avoid	71

B

bargain	55
be bound for	48
be full of	58
be sold out	65
belong to	37
belongings	70
beverage	58

block	89
book	43
branch	77
breakfast	23
broadcast	91
brochure	40
brush	22
budget	83
buffet	41
business trip	76

C

cancel	38
candidate	103
careful	71
carry	22
cash	53
celebration	97
cellphone	43
CEO	77
championship game	68
change trains	50
check in	44
circle	37
class	34
clearly	88
client	78
climb	22
cold	28
colleague	76
come up with	83

	commuter pass	46	e-mail address	26
	company	77	embassy	71
	concert	65	employee	77
	concierge	40	empty	59
	construction	89	event	68
	contract	85	exchange	43
	conversation	34	excited	65
	cool	52	exercise	29
	copier	77	expensive	52
	counter	40	**F** fail	73
	credit card	53	famous	64
	crowded	62	fare	47
	cure	28	fast-food restaurant	58
	customer	96	fever	28
D	daily life	26	fitting room	53
	data	82	for free	101
	deadline	34	forget	72
	degree	88	fork	58
	delay	47	**G** garden	22
	deny	72	grade	38
	department	86	gym	28
	departure time	47	**H** handout	82
	destination	47	hang	22
	details	96	happen	88
	discount	53	headache	28
	discovery	91	headline	99
	disease	31	headquarters	76
	dish	58	health	29
	do one's best	34	hire	76
	do the laundry	22	hobby	25
	document	80	homework	35
	dormitory	35	hospital	29
	downtown	89	hospitality	44
	due to	88	hotel	41
E	eat out	60	**I** in line	58

	information ········· 24			on TV ········· 65
	introduce ········· 82			order ········· 60
	itinerary ········· 41		**P**	parking lot ········· 50
J	job hunting ········· 86			part-time job ········· 25
K	knife ········· 58			passenger ········· 47
L	last ········· 64			passport ········· 70
	latest ········· 91			patient ········· 29
	lean ········· 22			pay ········· 53
	leave ········· 70			pay-phone ········· 40
	leave a message ········· 76			performance ········· 65
	library ········· 35			pickpocket ········· 71
	location ········· 25			pile up ········· 58
	look for ········· 52			popular ········· 65
	lose weight ········· 32			postpone ········· 72
	lost ········· 71			presentation ········· 83
	lost and found ········· 50			president ········· 76
	luggage ········· 41			prevent ········· 72
M	magazine ········· 99			price ········· 52
	major ········· 37			product ········· 97
	manager ········· 76			professor ········· 38
	manual ········· 77			profit ········· 86
	meal ········· 58			proposal ········· 82
	medicine ········· 28			purchase ········· 56
	meeting ········· 82		**Q**	quality ········· 96
	mention ········· 96			quit ········· 28
	mind ········· 72		**R**	raw fish ········· 62
	miss ········· 71			realize ········· 86
	move in ········· 26			reasonable ········· 52
	movie theater ········· 67			receipt ········· 53
N	news reporter ········· 90			reception desk ········· 40
	newspaper ········· 103			recover ········· 32
O	offer ········· 62			refill ········· 77
	office ········· 76			refund ········· 74
	on sale ········· 56			refuse ········· 73
	on time ········· 47			register ········· 53

remodel	97
rent	26
reserve	47
restroom	41
résumé	102
return	53
runny nose	29

S

sales representative	83
satisfy	62
scatter	58
school cafeteria	35
search	93
see a doctor	28
service charge	59
side by side	58
smoking	28
souvenir	41
spectator	68
stadium	64
station	50
stock	52
stomachache	29
strong	31
subject	35
submit	34
subway	47
successful	103
survive	93
sweep	22

T

take a day off	79
take a taxi	46
take place	34
tax	53
teeth	22
temperature	88
ticket	64
tip	59
tired	29
tour guide	44
tourist	40
traffic	88
traffic jam	89
transportation	47
travel agency	43
trip	47
trouble	70
try on	52

U

uniform	79
university	35
update	88
urgent	82

V

vehicle	89
vending machine	82
video game	64

W

wake up	23
warrant	96
water	22
weather	88
website	97
window seat	47
wonderful	68
wrap	53

Pre-test 解答用紙

Student ID	
フリガナ NAME 氏　名	

LISTENING SECTION

Part 1		Part 2		Part 3		Part 4	
No.	ANSWER A B C D	No.	ANSWER A B C	No.	ANSWER A B C D	No.	ANSWER A B C D
1	Ⓐ Ⓑ Ⓒ Ⓓ	3	Ⓐ Ⓑ Ⓒ	9	Ⓐ Ⓑ Ⓒ Ⓓ	18	Ⓐ Ⓑ Ⓒ Ⓓ
2	Ⓐ Ⓑ Ⓒ Ⓓ	4	Ⓐ Ⓑ Ⓒ	10	Ⓐ Ⓑ Ⓒ Ⓓ	19	Ⓐ Ⓑ Ⓒ Ⓓ
		5	Ⓐ Ⓑ Ⓒ	11	Ⓐ Ⓑ Ⓒ Ⓓ	20	Ⓐ Ⓑ Ⓒ Ⓓ
		6	Ⓐ Ⓑ Ⓒ	12	Ⓐ Ⓑ Ⓒ Ⓓ	21	Ⓐ Ⓑ Ⓒ Ⓓ
		7	Ⓐ Ⓑ Ⓒ	13	Ⓐ Ⓑ Ⓒ Ⓓ	22	Ⓐ Ⓑ Ⓒ Ⓓ
		8	Ⓐ Ⓑ Ⓒ	14	Ⓐ Ⓑ Ⓒ Ⓓ	23	Ⓐ Ⓑ Ⓒ Ⓓ
				15	Ⓐ Ⓑ Ⓒ Ⓓ		
				16	Ⓐ Ⓑ Ⓒ Ⓓ		
				17	Ⓐ Ⓑ Ⓒ Ⓓ		

READING SECTION

Part 5		Part 6		Part 7			
No.	ANSWER A B C D	No.	ANSWER A B C D	No.	ANSWER A B C D	No.	ANSWER A B C D
24	Ⓐ Ⓑ Ⓒ Ⓓ	32	Ⓐ Ⓑ Ⓒ Ⓓ	36	Ⓐ Ⓑ Ⓒ Ⓓ	44	Ⓐ Ⓑ Ⓒ Ⓓ
25	Ⓐ Ⓑ Ⓒ Ⓓ	33	Ⓐ Ⓑ Ⓒ Ⓓ	37	Ⓐ Ⓑ Ⓒ Ⓓ	45	Ⓐ Ⓑ Ⓒ Ⓓ
26	Ⓐ Ⓑ Ⓒ Ⓓ	34	Ⓐ Ⓑ Ⓒ Ⓓ	38	Ⓐ Ⓑ Ⓒ Ⓓ	46	Ⓐ Ⓑ Ⓒ Ⓓ
27	Ⓐ Ⓑ Ⓒ Ⓓ	35	Ⓐ Ⓑ Ⓒ Ⓓ	39	Ⓐ Ⓑ Ⓒ Ⓓ	47	Ⓐ Ⓑ Ⓒ Ⓓ
28	Ⓐ Ⓑ Ⓒ Ⓓ			40	Ⓐ Ⓑ Ⓒ Ⓓ	48	Ⓐ Ⓑ Ⓒ Ⓓ
29	Ⓐ Ⓑ Ⓒ Ⓓ			41	Ⓐ Ⓑ Ⓒ Ⓓ	49	Ⓐ Ⓑ Ⓒ Ⓓ
30	Ⓐ Ⓑ Ⓒ Ⓓ			42	Ⓐ Ⓑ Ⓒ Ⓓ	50	Ⓐ Ⓑ Ⓒ Ⓓ
31	Ⓐ Ⓑ Ⓒ Ⓓ			43	Ⓐ Ⓑ Ⓒ Ⓓ		

Post-test 解答用紙

Student ID	
フリガナ NAME 氏 名	

LISTENING SECTION

Part 1 No.	ANSWER A B C D	Part 2 No.	ANSWER A B C	Part 3 No.	ANSWER A B C D	Part 4 No.	ANSWER A B C D
1	Ⓐ Ⓑ Ⓒ Ⓓ	3	Ⓐ Ⓑ Ⓒ	9	Ⓐ Ⓑ Ⓒ Ⓓ	18	Ⓐ Ⓑ Ⓒ Ⓓ
2	Ⓐ Ⓑ Ⓒ Ⓓ	4	Ⓐ Ⓑ Ⓒ	10	Ⓐ Ⓑ Ⓒ Ⓓ	19	Ⓐ Ⓑ Ⓒ Ⓓ
		5	Ⓐ Ⓑ Ⓒ	11	Ⓐ Ⓑ Ⓒ Ⓓ	20	Ⓐ Ⓑ Ⓒ Ⓓ
		6	Ⓐ Ⓑ Ⓒ	12	Ⓐ Ⓑ Ⓒ Ⓓ	21	Ⓐ Ⓑ Ⓒ Ⓓ
		7	Ⓐ Ⓑ Ⓒ	13	Ⓐ Ⓑ Ⓒ Ⓓ	22	Ⓐ Ⓑ Ⓒ Ⓓ
		8	Ⓐ Ⓑ Ⓒ	14	Ⓐ Ⓑ Ⓒ Ⓓ	23	Ⓐ Ⓑ Ⓒ Ⓓ
				15	Ⓐ Ⓑ Ⓒ Ⓓ		
				16	Ⓐ Ⓑ Ⓒ Ⓓ		
				17	Ⓐ Ⓑ Ⓒ Ⓓ		

READING SECTION

Part 5 No.	ANSWER A B C D	Part 6 No.	ANSWER A B C D	Part 7 No.	ANSWER A B C D	No.	ANSWER A B C D
24	Ⓐ Ⓑ Ⓒ Ⓓ	32	Ⓐ Ⓑ Ⓒ Ⓓ	36	Ⓐ Ⓑ Ⓒ Ⓓ	44	Ⓐ Ⓑ Ⓒ Ⓓ
25	Ⓐ Ⓑ Ⓒ Ⓓ	33	Ⓐ Ⓑ Ⓒ Ⓓ	37	Ⓐ Ⓑ Ⓒ Ⓓ	45	Ⓐ Ⓑ Ⓒ Ⓓ
26	Ⓐ Ⓑ Ⓒ Ⓓ	34	Ⓐ Ⓑ Ⓒ Ⓓ	38	Ⓐ Ⓑ Ⓒ Ⓓ	46	Ⓐ Ⓑ Ⓒ Ⓓ
27	Ⓐ Ⓑ Ⓒ Ⓓ	35	Ⓐ Ⓑ Ⓒ Ⓓ	39	Ⓐ Ⓑ Ⓒ Ⓓ	47	Ⓐ Ⓑ Ⓒ Ⓓ
28	Ⓐ Ⓑ Ⓒ Ⓓ			40	Ⓐ Ⓑ Ⓒ Ⓓ	48	Ⓐ Ⓑ Ⓒ Ⓓ
29	Ⓐ Ⓑ Ⓒ Ⓓ			41	Ⓐ Ⓑ Ⓒ Ⓓ	49	Ⓐ Ⓑ Ⓒ Ⓓ
30	Ⓐ Ⓑ Ⓒ Ⓓ			42	Ⓐ Ⓑ Ⓒ Ⓓ	50	Ⓐ Ⓑ Ⓒ Ⓓ
31	Ⓐ Ⓑ Ⓒ Ⓓ			43	Ⓐ Ⓑ Ⓒ Ⓓ		

キリトリ線

| 教師用音声 CD 有り（非売品） |

GREEN LIGHT FOR THE TOEIC® TEST
やさしい TOEIC® テスト攻略入門

2016年3月1日　初版発行
2022年4月20日　第 7 刷

著　　　者　　土屋麻衣子、島居佳江、Samuel Paolo M. Adamos
発　行　者　　松村達生
発　行　所　　センゲージ ラーニング株式会社
　　　　　　　〒102-0073　東京都千代田区九段北1-11-11　第2フナトビル5階
　　　　　　　電話 03-3511-4392　FAX 03-3511-4391
　　　　　　　e-mail: elt@cengagejapan.com
　　　　　　　copyright ©2016 センゲージ ラーニング株式会社

装　　　丁　　（株）クリエーターズユニオン　森村直美
組　　　版　　有限会社ダイテック
編 集 協 力　　（株）WIT HOUSE
　　　　　　　　　　　ウィット　ハウス
印刷・製本　　（株）平河工業社

ISBN 978-4-86312-278-9

もし落丁、乱丁、その他不良品がありましたら、お取り替えいたします。
本書の全部または一部を無断で複写（コピー）することは、
著作権法上での例外を除き、禁じられていますのでご注意ください。